Letting the Lotus Bloom

The Expression of Soul through Flowers

Kevin Joel Kelly
Foreword by Thomas Moore

Llumina Press

ISBN: 978-1-62550-434-0

Dedicated to

My parents, Angelina and Gerald Kelly

Who loved flowers

Table of Contents

Foreword

Just as Alice's looking glass served as a portal through which she could enter new and different worlds, so each of us has at our disposal portals suited to us, magical entryways that reveal the depths of our world. In this deceptively simple and personal book by Kevin Kelly, the life of the florist and the practice of flower arranging becomes such a doorway to meaning.

I have known Kevin for a while now, and I know that he and I share certain values that are neglected in a society focused on making money and creating the hardware for a high-tech, high-functioning work force. Kevin and I place a higher value on beauty and the soft concerns of art. We both understand the importance of a beautiful arrangement of flowers at a funeral, a wedding, a party, or a small table at home by a window.

I have borrowed an outmoded word from the past for this appreciation of beauty and the tender emotions—soul. I have written with some complexity trying to apply ancient wisdom about the soul to our everyday lives. Kevin writes more directly from his own vision and experience, but his insights are no less valuable. In fact, I prefer to follow Kevin's personal history, his subtle observations of the place of flowers in the passages of a life, and his extraordinary ability to see simple daily events as metaphors and lessons for the greater issues of humanity.

The story is told of the Buddha that when he was asked to sum up his philosophy, he simply held up a flower. Some say this was the inspiration for the development of Zen. What an example of the creative power in a simple, delicate flower! Kevin has the Buddha nature. Instead of writing tomes on the meaning of life, Buddha-like he holds up his life as a florist for our contemplation and edification.

It is easy to romanticize flowers. Every time I use the word I feel a flush of sentimentality. But we need sentimentality, not sentimentalism, which is the abuse and exaggeration of tender feelings, to counter the harshness of the modern world. Plato said that education should include both music and gymnastics, so that the student would become neither too hard nor too soft. We could follow his insight and understand that our fascinating high-tech and speed-driven world has its own virtues, but it could use plenty of flowers, beautifully arranged, so as not to make our personalities metallic.

Every time I sit down to write about modern life, I think, too, of the ancient, rich tale of Narcissus, the boy whose body and countenance were like marble in their coldness and inexpressiveness. We live in a highly narcissistic society, which means that we find it difficult in this world to feel like somebody. We force the issue and try too hard to be noticed and to be higher in the pecking order. Our narcissism makes it difficult to be in community and have close friends.

In the story, Narcissus ultimately finds himself in a shaded grove at the side of a pond. At the moment of transformation, at his saving rite of passage, imagistically the tale says that he turned into a flower, specifically a daffodil. This story may be one of the most important for our times, and it is all about us becoming flower-like—tender, rooted, moist, delicate, beautiful. Kevin's book offers profound secrets that could help us in this necessary passage from stone-faced citizens to creative, floral individuals.

At my first glance at an early version of this book, I knew I wanted to offer it my support. As the world builds its weapons and transforms our cities with hard-edged, glassy skyscrapers, symbols of our narcissism, our uncertainty about our own worth, I see this book as a powerful antidote, the size of a seed perhaps, but nevertheless potentially transformative. I like everything about this book. It is couched in just the right portions of personal reflection and far-reaching ideas. It has the appropriate tenderness and beauty—certain words and phrases sprout up like soft pansies, a word which has long blended thoughts (pensée) and flowers. Like most good flower arrangements, it is subtle and complex.

There are those who will continue to use weapons to solve humanity's conflicts, but Kevin and I will go on our soft and silly ways, trusting the beautiful to educate the soul toward peace and creative expression. Jesus said, "Behold the lilies of the field." I try to behold them every day, and I behold this beautiful book, knowing that it offers more toward the healing of contemporary anxiety than all the burdensome expertise and all the hyperactive building that crowds our inner and outer space, leaving little room for the flowering of our landscapes and our souls. Let it teach you to arrange your life on the model of flowers artfully and gracefully set in a vase, transforming the world around them.

Thomas Moore

Introduction

Less than a year into my floral career a friend from college married a man from Japan. Immediately after the wedding, the couple moved to Japan, where they lived for two years. When they returned to Wichita they invited me to visit them at their lovely new home, and Janie regaled me with stories about their time in Japan. The one that struck me the most was about her weekly flower arranging lessons. She told me that in Japan people consider flower arranging to be a spiritual practice, a form of meditation. As she spoke, something opened inside of me and I realized that Western flower design held the same potential. But how? What was the connection between spirituality and flower arranging? The dialogue between my soul and art became the subtext of my career for the next three decades. And this book is a partial answer to that question about the connection between spiritual practice and flower arranging.

On some intuitive level, I'm fairly certain you already know what I mean. Flowers grace our days, enhance our celebrations, and comfort us in sorrow. When flowers enter a room they cast an enchantment that turns the ordinary into a moment of the extraordinary. People glow when they see flowers. Ever since I first became aware of flowers as a child, I have watched them cast their spell.

Flower arranging is a beautiful and very special art. Like all of the fine arts -- painting, sculpture, poetry -- flower arranging expresses the soul. But unlike many art forms, it holds its message only in the immediacy of today, because a flower arrangement doesn't last for long. Many of us live with a deep, innate longing to create. But often we sabotage ourselves because we think we have no "talent" or time, or can't afford to devote ourselves to something that can't earn us a living. What I have found and want to share with you here is that the creative life is built slowly. Like grains of sand making a beach, the accumulation of brief creative moments add up to the creative life. Acts of art do not stand alone, isolated from the rest of our lives. They teach us how to live creative, artful lives.

Why do so many of us feel called to create? Because the desire to pick up a crayon and draw or to place flowers in a vase is more than a whim; it is a call from the soul, a call to enter the inner sanctum, the place of imagination and intuition, thoughts and feelings, hopes and dreams.

And, from this mysterious inner realm, to bring forth fresh ideas and images.

Soul calls to us continually throughout our lives to live with its quality and depth, intimacy and conviviality. Soul beckons us to appreciate the goodness of life and to make use of its difficulties. Soul calls us to engage in activities, stillness, relationships, and solitude all for the purpose of birthing its quality in the world.

The calling of soul to art, whether it is to write a poem, make a painting, or arrange flowers, is the soul's yearning to become present through creation. It may present itself as a recurring idea or it may be a craving that draws us like a magnet.

I will not attempt to define soul; I will leave that to philosophers and theologians. For our purposes, soul needs no definition; it is readily identifiable. How many times do we hear the expression, "such soulful music," or "he or she has a great soul," or in contrast, "what a soulless job." No, rather than defining soul, my hope is that this little book will inspire a soulful *feeling*, a soulful *experience*.

There are many, many avenues for expressing soul's call. Mine happens to involve flowers because I find the art of flower arranging so elegant, so intuitive, so paradoxically simple and complex, so full of endless possibilities for artistic expression and the expression of soul. Placing a flower arrangement on a desk brings soul to an office, a rose on a dining table enhances the soul of a meal.

But the truth is, I can't teach you how to express soul or make art through flowers. The journey of creation is unique to each of us. What I *can* do is describe some of the techniques I use and try to inspire and encourage you to continue on the creative journey by telling you stories of some of my passages through acts of art. I will talk about the inner muscles of the creative life. What you do with this is up to you.

How This Book Came About

I began writing the book (birthing would be the more accurate verb) seven years ago. I was at a low ebb in my life, when I had to go to Alamosa, Colorado, to do the flowers for a wedding. The day before the wedding I woke up with the first line of this book buzzing in my head.

As I continued to write the book, I came to a strong image of what it was to become: a small, inspirational book, filled with the ideas I have gathered in over thirty years of flower arranging.

What does any of this have to do with the lotus? Throughout the world, the lotus has long been a symbol of inspiration and meditation, but I chose the lotus as the guiding image for this book simply because of its relationship to mud. Mud, complex and amorphous, troublesome and inconvenient, is the origin for the lotus' magnificent blossom. Art too springs from mud, the mud of the mind, the place of chaos.

If we want soul to be awakened like a lotus from its bud, we must be attentive to the ordinary moments of our lives. Soul lives in those moments like the lotus lives in the mud of a swamp. Beginning, like all flowers, as a small seed, the lotus digs its roots into the mud and releases its stem, leaves, and eventually its blossom to the sky. We who are artists can find meaning in the life of the lotus. Within each of us there is a blossom waiting to be born. As we struggle with the mud of our art and our lives, we give our blossom its opportunity for birth. It is a great paradox of art that as we create we are recreated and through the recreation, we blossom from within.

Rose

Chapter One

Flowers

I love flowers. They stream through my life like colors through a rainbow. Their gentle presence has been a constant source of satisfaction and inspiration.

I love dainty sweet peas and lily of the valley; fiery, bold ginger, protea, and heliconia; proud orchids; wild sunflowers and liatrice; simple daisies. I love exuberant pampas grass and timid violets, flirtatious dahlias and effervescent hydrangeas. I love the prickly texture of thistle and the tissue softness of rose petals. The spice scent of carnations and the sweet fragrance of gardenias are helium for my soul. I love an individual gladiola standing confident and tall, and I love arrangements that seem to hold multiples of every blossom under the sun. I love flowers! All of these and so many more.

For more than thirty years, flower arranging provided my livelihood, but my love affair with flowers began long before that. It weaves itself through my earliest memories.

My childhood home was a two-story beige duplex with brown trim and a red brick chimney. The front was faced with two story porches and was surrounded with white bridal wreath bushes. Old-fashioned purple iris lined the side, the kind of iris I always associate with grandmother. Cascading from a white trellis beside the back porch were scrumptious crimson roses, and across the driveway was a mock orange bush. All of these bloomed at approximately the same time each spring and for a moment I was in flower paradise. The rest of the yard and the rest of the year our property was a fifties drab blue grass lawn sprinkled with the occasional dandelion.

The little old lady two doors down, however, was another story. Now she was a gardener! (If I could see her now, as I am becoming the little old man down the street, I would probably not think of her as so old!) I loved visiting with her, as I ate the sour fruit from her cherry tree and enjoyed her garden displays. But things were not always so well between us.

In kindergarten, I discovered the wonderful ritual of May Day baskets. That spring on May 1st, I rolled small sheets of construction paper and glued on handles, just as I had learned in school. I then visited my neighbor's garden, and picked many of her spring blossoms to fill my baskets. Proudly, I presented a basket of iris, tulips, lilacs and daffodils to my Mother and one to Aunt Rose, who lived upstairs in the duplex. Then I proudly hung the rest on neighbors' doors.

I might have been spared the wrath of the gardener as well as my mother's punishment had I not tried to hang one on the gardener's door. As I quietly sneaked up to her door with the hopes of a happy surprise for her, the door flew open and she immediately marched me to my mother. The memory of my sore behind after that creative foray is still vivid. However neither the soreness nor the long-term banishment from the old lady's garden could dampen my passion for flowers.

I come by that passion honestly. My grandparents lived two hundred miles northeast of Kansas City in Mystic, Iowa. Grandpa Kelly was a renaissance man who supported his family of twelve children as a coal miner. Raising fancy pigeons, hunting, and gardening were high among his many interests. Gladiolas were the crowning glory of his garden. In my memory, they are a scene from an impressionist painting. An array of pink, yellow, purple, crimson, orange, red, and white stalks swaying in the Iowa breeze. I still dream, in sleep and awake, of his beautiful field of gladiolas.

He loved to share his flowers with others. Every Saturday, Grandpa made his rounds to the local churches, presenting big bouquets of glads to the church ladies to arrange for their Sunday services. During our visits I went with him. I remember the big smiles on the women's faces and his look of satisfaction as the gladiolas, his gift of good will, passed from his hands to theirs. It was communion before the communion services. Thus it was from my dad's dad that I inherited my love of flowers.

Childhood holds sweet dreams of passions waiting to be born. In those dreams we first meet our loves, joys, pleasures, and aspirations, which are like tender leaves in a spring garden. Our play holds hopes for our future as we glimpse the map to our maturity and take our first steps. And in those moments and activities, soul calls to us.

Chapter Two

An Invitation from the Flowers

When I arrived at the milestone of twenty-five years as a professional flower arranger, I wanted to celebrate with some fanfare, so I threw a party. I invited friends who appreciated and supported my work. A caterer provided a tea party bill of fare, which included finger sandwiches, scones and cream, assorted fresh fruits, and a variety of salads. My friend Wanda, a professional cateress, contributed a flower-laden cake and a barista from the local coffee shop brought his equipment and provided an espresso bar. A classical guitarist entertained in the living room, where a large bouquet of pink roses greeted my guests. The food was served buffet style in my library and there on the antique desk sat another large bouquet, this one of burgundy snapdragons, pink carnations, lavender cremons, heather, and purple statice. My home is a small 1920's bungalow but that evening the walls seemed to expand to create a mansion.

A local artist hand-printed the invitations. Most recipients responded to the invitation with enthusiasm, although a few seemed a bit miffed by the occasion. After all, I had not been at the same job all those years, nor was I retiring.

Their questions mirrored my own, since I was again reappraising my career, but intuitively I knew it was a moment to celebrate. I found the answer as the time for the party drew closer and I reflected on my relationship with flowers, savoring memories of a lifetime friendship. The invitation flowed from those reflections as I scribbled on a piece of scratch paper, "Roses, carnations, cremons, and their kin… For 25 years these have been my constant companions, warming my soul with nature's caress." "Yes!!!" I said, flowers have warmed my soul and shared their companionship in unassuming ways. As my friends, flowers have been consistent company and they have inspired my life.

Flowers are voiceless companions who continually share their wisdom and enhance our days. They shout for us to wake up when we are sleepy-eyed, ignoring the beauty of life. They teach us about the fragility of life and they tempt us to indulge in the pleasure of this moment for life is brief, they say, even at its longest. They remind us that in the complexity of life something as simple as a flower can be overlooked. They invite us to dance more fully with life.

One of the joys of friendship is this same quality. In my early years my friend Joe introduced me to classical music and thrift shops; Aunt Rose introduced me to opera and Aunt Evelyn to lamb and antiques; Shirley welcomed me to the new age; Tom led me to the dance floor; Charles introduced me to cultural highs of New York City, and Kenny to San Francisco; Jude brought the lotus into my life. And flowers encouraged me to pause for rainbows and to follow butterflies, and to grasp every available moment of beauty and hold those moments with white-gloved hands.

When I first wrote the party invitation, I knew in my heart the truth in the words that flowers "warmed my soul with nature's caress." They give me comfort when my heart breaks and they add their vitality to my celebrations, intensifying my joy. They sit beside me on quiet evenings when I curl up with a good book and they encourage me to explore my talents and give my spirit freedom to roam, to create, and to enjoy the day.

For all those years I thought I had been creating flower arrangements. What I now know is that as I was creating flower arrangements, flowers were recreating me.

Chapter Three

The Craft

I struggle learning the basics of almost everything in life from brushing my teeth to gardening and cooking. For instance, I once took a watercolor class. I arrived on the first evening with my head full of ideas for wonderful scenes I intended to paint, but I couldn't quite get loading the brush. While others were successfully painting onions I was still trying to get the right amount of pigment mixed with the right amount of water. Such technical details confound me.

Flower arranging was no different. My early years in flower shops were spent wrestling with the basics of the craft. Since then, I have watched many beginners, in classrooms and flower shops caught in the same struggles. I've also watched people fly right through the fundamentals, while others tried to ignore them altogether and create flights of fantasy. They produced one or two fascinating arrangements, but their work lacked consistency. The practice of the craft provides the opportunity to develop skills and promotes consistency, just the same as playing the piano, sewing clothes from a pattern, or cooking from a recipe.

The basics of the craft become the foundation for consistently successful and aesthetically pleasing flower arrangements. These are the building blocks of flower arranging and learning them is like learning the alphabet. After mastering the alphabet, words can be spelled, and with those words, poetry written. The more basic techniques and styles learned, the larger our floral vocabulary.

My professional career began humbly at Milady's Castle, the first mass marketer of flowers in Kansas City to place coolers in grocery stores and hospitals. Milady's Castle offered only three products, a package of six roses, a similar package of six carnations and a cellophane cylinder that held a small plastic goblet with an arrangement of five carnations. The cylinder defined the height and the pattern defined the placements of the carnations. There was a carnation on top, then two, and then three at the rim. Those crafted arrangements were turned out by the hundreds. While this was not a prestigious engagement, I was thrilled to be working with flowers and practicing the floral craft.

Just as playing the piano is more than pounding on the keys, flower arranging is more than plopping flowers in a vase. It is a fine art that is based on aesthetic principles. The craft of flower arranging involves learning certain patterns of flower arrangements and how to achieve those by controlling the flowers. The flower arranger must learn the primary elements of arrangement, such as line, form, and center, and become familiar with the flowers themselves, their textures, colors, weight, and flexibility. Craft allows the arranger to become competent at constructing arrangements from the ground up. In the craft of flower arranging, the success of an arrangement is judged by external criteria and relies on its proximity to the given pattern.

In craft, pattern is a general controlling the troops, but in the *art* of flower arranging, pattern, if it is present at all, becomes at most only a loose outline. In the art of flower arranging, judgment about which flowers to choose and what to do with them comes from the flower arranger her/himself.

When I started doing flower arranging for a living, I found the basics difficult to learn, but I also felt accomplished with each new technique or style I mastered. I was an eager student and, as I moved from flower shop to flower shop, I observed different designers at work, creating arrangements that inspired my own drive to accomplish. So I began to copy them. Helen at Crestwood Flowers designed the best inverted T arrangement I've ever seen. I stood and watched her and then copied. My lines were uneven and sloppy, while hers were precise, pristine and graceful, but I made progress. At Silver Flower Shop, Vicki did a triangular arrangement with the same exactitude. Truly a master of that shape, and others, her flowers cascaded in arrangements like a mesmerizing waterfall. There were others, too, and I am grateful to all of them for their patience and mentoring.

The craft provides the foundation and the springboard for the art. It takes a lot of practice, for there is much to master about shape and line and color and form. But the reward of practice is raw talent transformed into a dependable skill and a reliable consistency.

The soul is generous and seeks to pour itself out. It seeks to share its great treasures through many avenues including flower arranging. As we learn the craft we answer the soul's yearning by learning a vocabulary that gives soul a vehicle for expression. As the lotus is hidden in its seed, the art of flower arranging awaits its birth through the careful mastery of craft.

Sunflower

Chapter Four

From Craft to Art

I know the moment I transcend craft and create art. Craft's task is to copy what has been created and art's work is to create something new. The bridge between the two is imagination fueled by inspiration. Through the power of imagination we see beyond what is into what can become. We look at flour, sugar, eggs, and milk and see a cake; we gather iris, jonquils, daisies, astilbe and see an arrangement.

As we place the first flower from the imagination's picture, we enter the transcendent moment of art, the seminal moment of creativity. Now imagination births experience, and spirit marries matter, and soul enters the world via the artist.

Eighty miles north of Kansas City lies the Squaw Creek National Wildlife Refuge. There

15

in over seven thousand acres of marshes, bloom
legions of lotuses. It is a spiritual experience to
stand on the observation deck and witness them
wave to the heavens.

One year, I took a trip to Squaw Creek just
weeks prior to the blooming of the lotuses.
There was no hint of the muddy waters. Instead
I saw a sea of swaying green leaves. The light
played with the leaves, casting shadows, which
created the impression of a massive variegated
chenille throw. I wanted to curl into its comfort,
but knowing this was impossible, I let my spirit
romp through the leaves. Seeing the leaves of
the lotuses I could nearly see the blossoms yet
to come. As I stared at the leaves in quiet
reflection, they were already blooming in my
imagination.

The vision I saw of the blossoms was the
promise of the swamp that day. In much the
same way the imagination promises that no matter what is, more can be. When I look at a loose
assortment of flowers, my imagination sees the
arrangement. With my mind's eye, I see height,
depth, width, color, and form. I feel the intensity or gentleness of the arrangement. Its grace
or its sternness, its density or airiness, its softness or prickliness, stir in my imagination. The
image prods me to place the first flower.

I sat one pleasant spring afternoon with my
friend Lou and her daughter Kitty on Kitty's

patio where Lou and Al's golden anniversary celebration was to be held. We were there to discuss the party. At one end of the lawn the guests would dine at round tables under a tent, and at the other end, on the patio, the band would play. The caterer would serve the food in between and off to the side.

Lou requested only that I make arrangements for the tables, but as I sat with Lou and Kitty, sipping cappuccinos, my imagination began to roam. We discussed flower selection. I suggested that the centerpieces be composed of white roses, white snapdragons, golden aster and others yet to be selected. Lou said she loved daisies and Kitty agreed. Daisies could easily be incorporated into the centerpieces.

Lou also said that she loved sunflowers and white fugi mums, the latter I knew from making many arrangements with them for her over the years. Kitty commented on her love of gladiolas. We all agreed none of the three flowers were appropriate for the centerpieces.

Inspired by the setting, and Lou's love of those flowers, I wanted to use Lou's favorites. As I sat there, the undecorated emptiness that greeted guests captured my attention. The lawn was lovely and Kitty was planting some nice garden pots, but there was nothing that visually carried the sense of celebration from the entrance back to the tent. To remedy this I imagined a large arrangement in the middle of the lawn that included sunflowers, fugi mums, and gladiolas. They agreed. Next, in my mind's eye, I saw pictures of free form arrangements made of matching flowers suspended from the trees. My design for Lou's party was complete and I knew that the flowers would carry the eyes of the guests from the gate to the tent and would herald a sense of celebration. When I made the arrangements I used all the flowers we discussed plus golden oncidium orchids. From the reactions of the guests, I knew that the pictures from my imagination were right on target.

In preparation for the act of art, I seek inspiration, the fuel of the imagination. A container may suggest the flowers, the accoutrements that will sit with it on the table may suggest the shape, and the room may direct the choice of colors. At times a flower itself begs an ensemble.

Often a discussion will inspire my arrangements. When I am working with a bride, for instance, I listen for the mood and atmosphere she desires for her wedding. Will it be a bombastic celebration? Or perhaps a quiet, intimate affair? Does she want the flowers to reflect the majesty of the forest, the dignity of a formal garden, or the whimsy of a wild flower field? As I listen to her discuss her dreams and plans I become inspired and then my imagination begins to see the flower arrangements for her wedding.

I also reap inspiration by visiting the place flowers are to be used. The room, or church, or garden, encourages ideas and spawns fantasies that translate into floral art. In my minds eye I look for ways that flowers will join with the surroundings to enhance the celebration.

If I leave my imagination free to roam wild, mental pictures always come. They may or may not be realistic, but they bear a sense of the possibilities for the arrangements. Sometimes these pictures reveal themselves over a period of time and sometimes in a flash. This process feels like pure magic!

Though imagination shows an arrangement complete before begun, the image in the mind's eye is only a blueprint. As the arrangement is created, it will take on a life of its own and each step of the way the imagination will send updates guiding the act of art.

As I enter the transcendent moment and begin creating a flower arrangement mental debates cease. It is in this moment, as inspiration guides imagination through my hands, that I transcend the craft and create art. Now in sublime surrender to creative power, the arrangement comes through me.

Artists are inspired people and inspiration is mother's milk for our souls. We thrive on that glimmer of an idea, a glimpse of a possibility, some shooting star that enflames our passions.

We are people who keep company with the muse. Often we make her acquaintance when we are in love. We look at the beloved and our hearts overflow with poetry. But as we mature we hear her voice in the leaf that glides on a breeze, the horns honking in a traffic jam, a delectable pastry, or a line of poetry that hits a nerve like a dentist drill on an undeadened tooth. She calls to us in pain and pleasure alike and demands that we create.

This is the vitality of artists' lives. Through inspiration we glimpse an idea, through imagination we dream how we can use that idea, and then, through the transcendent moment, we create. We marry a daisy with a dahlia, not because of a command from a pattern, but because we heard the whisper of the muse.

When I look at a flower arrangement where the artist has transcended the craft, I see the art. It is in the composition as a whole and in the subtlety of the details. The quality of an arrangement is seeable and measurable and rests on a blend of masterful skills learned in the craft with the artistry of arranging.

The soul prods us to create through our imaginations. When we follow that prodding and enter the transcendent moment of art we stand in the presence of the sacred.

Chapter Five

Spiritual Practice

How does an empty vase become a display of summer's fire with golden sunflowers, fiery red celosia, hot pink dahlias, and purple coneflowers? By trusting the transcendent moment. As we learn to trust the transcendent moment we learn to trust our own souls. Acts of art are proving grounds for this trust, as we awaken to the idea via the imagination and then give it form, dimension, texture and color.

Art opens the door to the world of possibilities that lies within each of us, and it teaches us how to navigate there. Then it moves the lesson into the material world.

The world of the imagination is crowded with ideas, some are useless and others are possibilities waiting to be born. Imaginative ideas are like the first sprouts in a spring garden where it can be difficult to distinguish between the flowers and the weeds. One spring early in my gardening career, frustrated from an overabundance of weeds, I diligently plucked hundreds of little sprouts from my garden only to realize I had taken out all the Missouri primrose and left all the ragweed.

Flower arranging has taught me to be both eager for the idea and skeptical at the same time. I trust my imagination, but true to my Missouri roots, I want to be shown. I want to know that the idea I'm grasping has merit. The ability to discern the flowers from the weeds grows through practice. After all it doesn't take many toppled vases caused by flowers that were too tall or too heavy to understand the idea of proportion and balance. Now, if I have a delicate six-inch vase and my mind's eye suggests a thirty-inch gladiola I know to reject the idea and find a taller vase for the gladiola or a shorter flower for the vase such as a tulip that will entertain for days bending, twisting, and turning as it dances with the light.

As we practice we refine our abilities to discern workable ideas, we hone our skills, and we learn to take the transcendent moment and cultivate it, compromise with it and to keep the dialogue running between the psyche and the experience.

This spiritual practice does not flow from a theology; rather it flows from working with the relationship of the unseen to the seen. And rather than remaining in lofty philosophical ideology it allows itself to be proven in the microcosm of a flower arrangement. Best of all, for every creative challenge, every empty vase, there is a myriad of possibilities that allow us to learn by trial and success.

Just as nature blooms and returns to rest through four seasons, the spiritual practice of soulful art has four phases. They are phase one, practicing the craft, phase two, the transcendent moment, phase three, mind chatter and experimentation, phase four, surrender.

In phase one, the craft, we put the fundamental techniques of craft to work. We select the flowers and container, choose a form, and decide on the mechanics. For instance we may choose a low bowl for a centerpiece and then soak and tape the floral foam. We then begin cutting the flowers to an appropriate size and place them according to the form we want to create.

In phase two, the transcendent moment is the threshold where the imaginative world touches the material world. The transcendent moment happens as we create our flower arrangement. For instance sometimes as I make a traditional Christmas centerpiece, similar to hundreds I have made before it, I place the candle, and the first evergreen boughs, and then suddenly my imagination takes over and I am passing through the transcendent moment. Then where I was going to place a few red carnations, my imagination has selected instead roses and berries. The transcendent moment drives the act of art and as we engage in it, we may pass through the transcendent moment time and again. Half the work of creation is done in the vase and half within our own minds.

In phase three, mind chatter and experimentation we look at each stem and ask should it be placed here or there? Does it even belong? What color is missing, which color is overwhelming? The list of questions can be long as we choose each flower until we are satisfied. During this phase I have looked at a nearly completed arrangement, been dissatisfied with it, torn it apart, and begun again. Here is where our ability to discern the value of ideas is practiced.

In phase four, surrender, the act or art flows through us like breath through a flute. Like a Buddhist chanting or a Catholic reciting "Hail Marys" the act of art paces itself and pours from our souls. Here we turn from all our preconceived notions and release them so something new can be created in the moment, born from soul.

I still remember clearly, learning to ride my bike. I received my shiny red and silver Schwinn for my sixth birthday. My dad immediately took me out to the sidewalk around our house for instruction. Our home on a corner lot was surrounded on two sides with a three-foot rock retaining wall that I could lean into if I began to fall. My dad patiently walked with me, holding on to the bike and helping to steady me. Though I was acquiring the requisite number of bruises and scratches, I was determined to ride because I knew from watching the other kids, that once I could ride propelled by my own power, I could soar. Eventually, in the twinkling of an eye and unbeknownst to me, my dad let go, and sure enough I soared. Each phase in the spiritual practice of art has its honored place and as we practice we will come to a moment when we soar.

This is a skeletal view of this spiritual practice. The other chapters of this book will add flesh, but the full body is experienced in the hours we spend engaged in the practice whether with one medium or many, whether writing, painting, flower arranging, homemaking, or gardening. Each day is fertile with opportunities to pass through the transcendent moment in creative acts.

As we grow in spiritual practice, it entwines our lives like morning glories on a fence and brings with it the fragrance of the divine. As we engage in art, we touch our souls through imagination and we birth soul in the world through our hands. Like a daisy chain, hand connects to soul connects to mind. This is the inner sanctum of creativity, the holy of holies that deserves our respect and earns our trust. In this holy act we meet the mystery that lies within our souls, the mystery that always awaits another birthing.

Chapter Six

The Mud

We live in a society that roars for our attention. Family, community, and jobs shout their demands and enticements. As we make commitments to these, responsibilities mount, usurping our time and energy. We are lured by advertisements and peer pressure to possess everything from the right deodorant to the perfect car, from the largest house our money will stretch to buy, to the latest technology without regards for our deeper needs that may be drowned by all these possessions.

Where do we give our time and attention first, second and last? How will we spend our money, and how do we fulfill our hopes dreams and desires when so many others are demanding so much from us?

Things don't always go so well and often we are mired in conflict as our finest ideas and dreams are shot down by others and by circumstances. At other times no one stands in the way of the fulfillment of our dreams or plans and yet failure comes in spite of our best efforts.

The clock sets the pace of our lives as we awake in the morning with the best of intentions for what we will accomplish. Unexpected traffic jams, or an emergency trip to the dentist, or excessive telephone calls thwarted all our best intentions. Then we go to bed frustrated by our failure to accomplish it all.

People die, marriages dissolve, friendships fade, and fortunes, big and small, are lost. Daily irritations at work and in the family drive us to distraction. At times, life is crowded with disagreeable moments, people, and events.

Altogether this is the mud of life – the collage of adventures and misadventures, the happenings and the mishaps of our lives that absorb our attention, abscond with our time, and devour our feelings. If we look deeply into the mud of our lives we will be confronted with the confusion, chaos, and complexity of our existence. It is the mud that sends people to ministers' offices, therapists' couches, and support groups, and that fills coffee shops with people in empathic conversation. Patrons seeking relief from the mud of their lives also pay for many bar stools.

The mud exists around us and is echoed within, and does not go away. Sometimes it is more expansive and at other times it nearly disappears, but to a greater or lesser degree, it is always present. For the lotus the constant presence of the mud is good news because the lotus depends on the mud for its life. This is true for our lives as well. The dilemma we face is how to use the mud because when we use it well, it grips and secures us. When we figure out how to stand in the chaos without being swallowed whole, we discover our strength. When we fail to use it we risk being used by it and then it grips us to strangulation.

It is easy when we become mired in the mud to become deafened to soul's call and to lose sight of our creative potential. However, into this confusion, soul will send its tender roots as it seeks a home and from this mud something beautiful will sprout. Soul is persistent in issuing its call and if we pay attention to our desires, enthusiasms, and dreams, the mud will serve a purpose as it challenges us to our best. For a vital creative life we need to look at the mud that surrounds us and remember that the mud serves the lotus.

Soul thrives in the mud of our lives with its complexity and confusion. The complexity and confusions is mirrored in the complexity of flower arranging. On the rare occasion that I have a dinner party, I will make a centerpiece for the table. First I select a bowl, usually china or pottery so I can use floral foam without struggling to hide it. Then I go to the cooler to select my flowers. Here is where I most clearly face the complexity. I stare at the buckets of carnations, roses, gladiolas, larkspur, Asian lilies, rubrum lilies, alstromeria, chrysanthemums, snapdragons, and the vases of freesia, iris, tulips, gerbera daisies, daffodils, heather, statice, hydrangeas and on and on—so many choices and my bowl is so small. But I come to the cooler with the intention of a spring centerpiece. So I easily eliminate the red rover mums, orange carnations, and bronze poms. My imagination begins to call for my selection. The freesia and tulips will make a lovely beginning and their size will work well in my centerpiece because I will want to keep my arrangement low so my guests can converse without straining over or around the flowers.

All of these considerations, from the choice of container to the selection of flowers to the height of the arrangement demonstrates the process of sifting through the complexity of options as we are guided by imagination and intuition to make choices. This, too, is how soul uses the complexity of our lives. Through its call, it helps us to know what to take with us from the mud and what to leave behind.

The exact contents of the mud is unique to each of us, but the mud of artists' lives often share a common element: pervasive negative messages about creativity and the importance of its role in the human drama. How often I have heard a mother or father bemoan a child's dream by saying "all he or she wants to be is an *arteest*," the very mutilation of the word belittling the creative.

Constantly I hear the stories of discouraged artists drained by soulless jobs because they needed to pay the bills. In a world that too often values conformity over creativity, artists often feel marginalized and isolated, and fall prey to discouragement. In the extreme, artists walk completely away from their art. This represents a great loss of soul for themselves and the community. This is a complex problem with no easy solution.

I have lived this complexity and my career as a florist began in it. I spent my four years of high school and one year of college in a Catholic seminary. I left college and the seminary and returned to live with my parents. My father was unemployed at the time and my mother was disabled from a back injury. My father insisted that I find a job immediately and to that end he got me hired on at a tennis racket factory in a minimum wage position.

The owner used intimidation and harassment to control his crew. Each morning he randomly selected an employee to stand on a table in the center of the factory surrounded by all his coworkers. There the boss berated him with vicious comments for some mistake, usually miniscule, that the employee had made on the previous day. Everyday I went to work terrified that it would be my day.

My job was to load and unload the rackets from a computerized machine that punched the holes for the strings. My responsibilities included accurately setting the machine so that the holes were properly spaced on the rackets. Unfortunately for him and me, he was the one who trained me and his training left me confused. Then, when I requested that he show me again, he made certain I knew it was my last chance to learn.

I never asked another question. Each day I loaded and unloaded the machine, aware that the rackets were misdrilled. After three weeks and thousands of misdrilled tennis rackets, I was called to his office where I quit and was fired all in the same split second. I was relieved and my father was furious. He demanded an immediate decision about my next step to gainful employment. Without thought I replied that I was going to be a florist. I still find it interesting how quickly I made that decision, I who can spend days deciding what to put on a grocery list.

That job at the tennis racket factory was a soul killer, but the experience as well as the feelings of desolation and failure became part of the mud of my life. That mud experience opened my ears to hear soul's call to creativity through flower arranging. I took the job at the tennis racket factory because my father called me to go to work and make money; I became a florist because deep within I heard soul's call to a life dedicated to creation.

Just as it is difficult to walk in mud, it is difficult to struggle with the mud of our lives whether it is the outer noise or our own inner turmoil. However, as an athlete's body is refined by exercise, we are refined through the struggle as we choose to follow the call of our souls. Through this struggle we identify our desires, own our passions, speak down to naysayers, and liberate our talents.

How we use the mud and how we respond to soul's call is individual to each of us. It is not important whether we create for hobby or hire. Nor is this an either/or situation. Rather it is a matter of giving creation a place of honor at the tables of our lives.

As we create, regardless of the medium, soul is birthed. No matter how loud the noise that would draw us away from creation, it is always our choice to follow or ignore soul's call. But it is a choice that deeply affects the quality of our lives and the lives of our communities.

We can learn from children who take pleasure in the mud as they make mud pies. They welcome rainy days and the ensuing mud. We too can welcome the mud of our lives as we accept its challenges and struggles because through the mess of the mud, soul is creating people committed to creation. People who like the lotus draw nourishment from the mushy, heavy mud in the swamp that teems with vitality.

Too often as adults we prefer to ignore mud, as we sidestep it to keep our shoes from getting dirty, but the mud of our lives cannot be ignored if we want to have the qualities of soul in our art and in our lives. While I may not like it, I have learned to love the mud of life as well as the blossom of the soul–the two are directly connected. After all, life, like a swamp, is messy. Soul neither praises nor deplores the mess, nor does it remove us or redeem us from it. Instead, it uses the mud of our lives to bring us to our blossom.

Tulip

Chapter Seven

Voice and Intuition

For many of my years as a flower arranger I searched for my style. I asked trusted friends, "Do you think I have an identifiable style?" Their answers were always an emphatic yes. But I looked at my work and saw no connecting thread, no one-signature element that identified my arrangements as my own.

I struggled with this until I became aware that I realized my voice in flowers arranging. Long before I recognized it, my voice, with its unique timbre, flowed through my arrangements, allowing my soul's presence. In nature's symphony every bird has its melody and in the great chorus of human expression, every artist has a voice. The artist's voice is the channel of the soul's intent and presence just as the stem of the lotus carries life from the seed to the blossom.

It was a struggle to identify my voice, because just as overbearing streetlights can make the stars invisible, the cacophony of this noisy world nearly drowned out my voice. The noise was not only the clamoring in the outer world; it was also the ranting of my own mind.

But as I worked with flowers, I discovered that the passion and care conveyed through a flower arrangement is the presence of the voice of the artist. When I arrange an altar gushing with forsythia, blue iris, pink roses, and lilacs, then softened and blended with baby's breath brings the light spirit of a spring garden to a May wedding just as surely as if fairies themselves danced there, my voice is heard. An exuberant centerpiece at a birthday dinner that accentuates the celebration like fireworks on the fourth of July is echoing the celebration of my soul. Such is the magic of the art of flower arranging.

Part of my soul work has had to do with becoming comfortable with silence. In the quiet of comforting spaces, such as gardens, parks, chapels, and home, I could disengage from the static of the cacophony. Through the wisdom of good books, and in the silence of meditation, I came to know the themes of my heart and soul. In soft conversations and gentle friendships I heard the echoes of those themes. And as I became conscious of them flowing from my soul into arrangements, I awoke to the hymn of my voice.

When we try to search for our voice, consciously, deliberately, voice can be elusive. But it sprouts naturally when we follow the intuitive nudges of our souls to engage in acts of art. Like the first crocus of spring, the intuitive thought appears as though from nowhere. If we listen, intuition, rooted in mystery, guides our hearts, our minds and our hands. Like a shooting star in a still night sky, intuition erupts from inner vision.

One day a family came into the flower shop and placed an order for the funeral flowers for the matriarch of their family. Although I did not meet with these people, I made the arrangements. For their tribute the family had requested yellow and pink roses, blue iris, and lavender tulips and they also suggested that the designer could add other flowers. Since I was to make the piece, I went to the wholesale market to select the flowers for their arrangement. As I shopped, my eyes kept returning to a bouquet of yellow enchantment lilies, which seemed to beg to be included in their arrangement.

The next day, after the piece was completed, two more members of the family came in to place another order. When they heard that the family arrangement was finished they asked to see it. I was not the one waiting on them, but since I had arranged the piece my employer requested that I show it to them. They took one look at it and one of them exclaimed, "Yellow lilies, they were Mother's favorite!" I have had many such experiences. They encourage me to continue to listen to my intuition and to then express my thoughts and feelings in flower arrangements.

Intuition is an important tool in the artist's hand. It is the idea in the gut or the craving in the mind.

Intuition inspires our voices and as we continue to follow it, our voices will sound through our flower arrangements.

Our intuition can hit us over the head or whisper in our ear. The intuitive thought can come from a conversation, or a passage in a book, from something we see, such as the yellow lilies, or from what seems like no place at all. As a matter of a fact it can float in anywhere, any time, from any place.

Discerning the value of an intuitive thought is a must because sometimes it is right on target, at other times it can be so off base it is unusable. More often it is an idea we give shape and form to like clay in the potter's hands. It is important that we always remember that an intuitive idea is the beginning of the discussion not the final word. In fact the act of art itself discerns the value of the intuitive thought. As we make our arrangements, we will come to know what is working and what should be rejected. In the end the work of art is the final word on the value of the intuitive thought.

Too many atrocities are committed and too many stupid acts perpetrated because someone failed to discern the value of intuitive thought. By the same token, too many acts of art and good deeds go undone because someone walked away from the intuitive thought. Intuition is one vital aspect of the act of art that is weighed and balanced with the other aspects just as the lotus is just one element of a swamp.

Chapter Eight

Lines, Form, Lineage

S treets, whether straight or winding, hold the body of a city and make it accessible. In the same way that streets hold a city, lines hold the arrangement, establishing the height, depth, breadth, and flow. By establishing lines, one moves through an arrangement, just as by establishing streets, one moves through a city.

When we approach a vase or container, it is an empty vessel, containing only space. As we begin to create an arrangement the line establishes the relationship of the arrangement to the container, as it secures the arrangement in its place. As it travels from the container, the line also establishes the relationship of the arrangement to its place in the room.

The lines of an arrangement may be simple, such as one vertical and one horizontal in an inverted T arrangement or as an S line in a Hogarth curve, or there may be many lines meandering through an arrangement creating an exuberant work like string confetti at a birthday party. Lines may be readily visible, or they may be hidden in the complexity of the arrangement, barely noticeable. We may first establish the line and then hang the arrangement on it, or we may establish the line as we build the arrangement. Either way the line creates the structure that establishes the strength of the arrangement and if we are adventuresome, we allow it to take us places in the arrangement we never dreamed.

For instance, I may be creating a piece to sit in front of a mirror on a credenza using ginger to establish a substantial height that will accentuate the rhythm of the lines of the mirror's edge and lead the eye higher where it will catch the reflection of the chandelier that appears to hover above. Then I may establish a strong horizontal line with many strands of ivy that carries the eye to an art object that will share space on the credenza, when suddenly the line wants to become a series of circles cascading from the credenza while other strands vine up along the mirror. Such a diversion has caused the arrangement to change from the intense formal arrangement that I had planned to a nearly comical overgrowth of ivy that reminds me of my own garden.

Now to offset this change of plans I will have to respond throughout the rest of the arrangement with a placement of flowers that lightens the mood of the entire piece and relaxes the initial sternness of the ginger.

While the line establishes the structure and direction of the arrangement, its form defines the overall shape that hangs on the line; it is the flesh and muscle that completely covers the skeleton allowing the lines to make sense. It is the nosegay covering a circle, or the cascade encompassing a falling line in a bridal bouquet. The form establishes the boundaries of the arrangement. The line places the tip, and establishes the flow of the flowers, but the form establishes the arrangement's edges.

In contrast, a free form arrangement ignores the anticipated edge as the flowers extend beyond the core form that lies hidden within the arrangement. As we move beyond the established outline in free form style the other aspects of flower arranging, such as balance, scale, rhythm, and space become increasingly important so that all the elements appear to belong to the ensemble.

But first we must have line and form. Line and form are the basic underpinnings of an arrangement. They allow us to establish a direction from which we can then take flight to create a fantasy as we explore its terrain. Giving the arrangement its physical reason for being, they secure its place in the container and establish its roots and its history as the first flower flows to the last.

41

Our lives have lines, too, basic themes that give direction and hold the flesh of our souls. Some are constantly present, others fade and re-appear as they weave themselves through the complexity of our lives. Lines composed of recurring dreams and fantasies, hopes and passion, direct our interests and inspire our continuing projects, involvements, and commitments.

Each one of us comes from a biological lineage or line that includes ancestors and relations.

However, we also have ancestors and relations of the soul; those who are creative, philosophical, and spiritual kin. As we look at our lives and become acquainted with the callings of our souls we will discover some of them. We recognize them when we hear their stories, or experience their art, and we feel our souls leap with enthusiasm. As we hear the stories of other creatives, contemporary and from many centuries past, and we find ourselves exhilarated, then we know we have found other members of our line. Looking to those who have come before us and stand beside us helps us understand ourselves better. The stories of others in our lineage who pursued their calling can inspire us to contribute our own genius to the world.

If we question whether or not our souls are artist souls, all we have to do is look at the history of our enthusiasm. What stories sparked passion, what persons inspired dreams, what activities generated fervor? The answers to those questions give hints to the nature of our own souls.

We can beckon our ancestors through our imagination, allowing them to inspire our minds and hearts as we welcome their company and grace. For instance, my mother's family came from Italy and I often picture them there. The image of my Italian kin helps sustain me. Throughout my career, I have also held a rich image of a Master flower arranger in Japan. I see him making his arrangements, tending his garden, teaching flower arranging, sipping tea, and writing poetry. He has been a guiding light as I cultivated my life and my art.

We may know very little about our ancestors. That doesn't matter. It is not necessary for us to be able to place a date and a time on an ancestor's life to imagine that he or she lived. Many may live only from our imaginations, speaking truths that inspire our lives and bestow on us the blessing of generations as we respond to the calls of our souls.

Just as a line establishes the relationship of the arrangement to the container, our lineage establishes our relationship to life and culture. Others who have gone before us and imbued life with their gifts have made ready a place for us.

I have often felt lonely in my creative pursuits as I walked alternative paths that took me far beyond the recognized "norm" of life that many around me, particularly my biological family, seemed to be living, and I have watched and talked with other artists who questioned their paths because of the same loneliness. But as we look to the lines of our lives as well as to the creative lineage from which we come, we can appreciate the call to destiny that we follow, just as the line of the lotus extends from its roots, through its stem, to its blossom.

Chapter Nine

From Chaos to Completion

One day, while attempting a mad dash from the house, I realized I didn't have my reading glasses, which usually dangle from a chain around my neck. The search was on! I rifled through drawers and cabinets; I dumped baskets and toppled piles of papers; on tiptoe, I reached high and, on my hands and knees, I searched low. Finally, after a good thirty minutes and totally exasperated, I threw up my hands and there they were, entwined in my keys, clutched in my left hand.

It seems as though, in the confusion of my chaotic spaces, I spend half my life searching for glasses, keys, bills, or my cap. My desk is a mountain of papers and miscellaneous bric a brac, and the sock drawer in my dresser currently contains old travel brochures, empty cologne bottles, a book, extra toothbrushes, and two handkerchiefs, scrunched up receipts, and no socks! They are strewn throughout the other drawers. I will leave the contents of my closets and cupboards to the imagination.

I am the same way in my work. As I arrange, I tend to pile flowers and greens beside me, buckets surround me, and skyscrapers of discarded stems lay beneath my feet. I am constantly searching for my knife, since my tools are usually lost somewhere at the bottom of the heap. While I love the aesthetics of a well-ordered area, I find it difficult to work if my area is too neat because the chaos triggers my creative acts.

Chaos holds a kaleidoscopic beauty that fascinates my imagination. Like a little boy with a pile of tinker toys, I step into the pandemonium and become architect of my world. I stand looking at the disparate pieces wondering what will be, fascinated by the possibility as they call for order, just like scattered pieces of a jigsaw puzzle begging assembly.

The chaos around me mirrors the chaos in my mind and heart. As I begin my work I feel the angst of the diverse bits and pieces of my inner thoughts and feelings as they free float. What flowers will I use? Which container? Will they all work together; will they satisfy the needs and wants of the person the flowers are intended for? And if they are for myself will they satisfy my aesthetic needs at that moment? Sometimes I need the ferocity of what appears to be a man-eating protea, at other times I need the gentle cascade of vining sweetpeas. I stand staring at the materials, eager to begin and wanting to run away. I worry as I wonder if I am enough to succeed at this project, and yet at the same time I am enthused at the opportunity to prove myself again. The chaos rages at many levels and I question myself and the pieces of the puzzle until I begin. The spin of the kaleidoscope works its magic and the pieces become the whole.

In fact, the chaos presents the challenge and stimulates the fun. No matter how well ordered a workplace itself is, whether that is a flower shop, a kitchen, or a potting shed, the arrangement begins in chaos. As we peruse our assortment of flowers, greens and containers, whether they are cuttings from our gardens or buckets of flowers purchased at a wholesale house or an assortment of blossoms from a flower shop, like a child with a pile of tinker toys, we make a selection and begin.

Sometimes I choose the container first and sometimes the flowers, but whichever, I most often begin the arrangement with layers of greens. I still prefer to arrange using floral foam over a vase with just water because I can use a wider selection of containers and create a greater range of styles, so generally the perfunctory reason for greening in is to cover the foam. However, by greening in first, I marry the arrangement to the container, as I allow foliage to overlap its edges.

It can be quite enough to use only one variety of greens such as leather leaf, lemon leaf, or camellia foliage, but when a variety of foliages are used an arrangement has a head start for becoming a more fascinating arrangement since each different foliage will add varying shades of green, as well as an array of shapes and textures.

As the foliage becomes denser, and as the foliage and the container become a single unit, the foundation for the arrangement is established. A strong foundation supports the arrangement and keeps the eye in the arrangement, even as the flowers and branches soar, leading the eyes skyward. As well, as the greens take shape, they will suggest the form for the arrangement.

Once the foundation is complete I begin adding flowers. I often let the individual flowers speak, I even let them take the lead. I may intend to place a gladiola or liatrice, when a ginger begs to be placed. Such a strong flower in itself, it needs support to be brought back down to the foundation, so I will shadow it with another or perhaps with the liatrice, stair stepping them down from the first ginger. Then a king protea seems the ideal flower to cut short and place at the base. This creates an enthralling tension for the eyes, as they are taken to the outer limits of the arrangement with the ginger, and yet brought back and anchored by the protea. One flower at a time, the chaotic array of flowers from miscellaneous vases and piles around my worktable becomes a completed arrangement.

Like that little boy with the tinker toys, I am thrilled by the pile and proud of the finished construction, but the fun was in the building, one block at a time. I find that after sifting through the diverse elements of chaos, and then building the arrangement to completion, what I see with my eyes satisfies my soul.

Of course there is a flip side here, too. I am often amused by the chaos in my work area and in my life, but sometimes I suffer from it. I suffer from those lost precious minutes searching for my glasses, or from the late charges on lost bills. I suffer the insult when my chaos is public and it is ridiculed or dismissed as sloppiness. I need to know that the suffering caused by the myriad of loose strands in my life counts for something.

Flower arranging is a ritual that reminds us that something beautiful can come from the scattered fragments of our lives and that the cycle of life spins ever on from chaos to completion. The vitality of the Lotus is evidenced in its cycles and the vitality of our creative lives is seen likewise, as we complete works of art begun in the rawness of chaos.

Cymbidium Orchids

Chapter Ten

Resistance and Power

I love to swim and many years ago I swam a mile a day. As I approached the pool, I always felt a little shiver at the thought of the cool water. That shiver was the voice of resistance. Then one day I walked to the edge of the pool, felt the shiver, and headed for the hot tub. It was years before I swam again. During those years I surmised that I had simply grown tired of the daily swimming regimen. Then one day I was in a discussion on resistance with a group of friends and the inner bells and whistles went off as I realized that I had quit swimming because I had given in to resistance. I returned to the pool and swimming once again became a regular part of my exercise.

Resistance is that bratty little voice that says, "I don't wanna, and I'm not gonna!" It can feel like laziness, disregard, discontent, or even dread.

Procrastination is a warning sign that resistance is involving itself in our business. We hear that voice, "Sure, I'll do it, just not now." Resistance may show up as a dead end, but more often than not, it presents itself as a detour. I know that I often resist my creative urges. Somehow I find it much easier to find the solitaire games on my computer than the word processing, and walking into the flower shop I can find a dozen trivial tasks to occupy myself so I can avoid picking up my knife and creating an arrangement. Or the vase is prepared, the flowers are selected, the knife is in my hand, I am ready to go, and all of a sudden I need a coffee break. That is resistance. Left unchallenged, resistance becomes a nearly insurmountable block as our potential acts of art become mired in a quagmire of excuses.

Just as a single project, arrangement, or day of work can be resisted, so too, can the inner work that art demands. Like a locked door to a home, resistance guards the inner contents of an artist's psyche and when resistance is released, the contents are accessible. There we find our hopes, dreams, talents, desires, ambitions, and expectations, as well as our history, our emotions, motivations, regrets, and faults. This is the deep pool of ourselves, and art demands we take a sacred responsibility for what we find there.

The responsibility of art is to use what we find in our depths for the purpose of creation. With art, nothing is wasted, no tragedy, no celebration, no emotion. Like the scraps in a collage, art draws on the fragments of our lives and makes something new in an ever-evolving cycle, just like the seasons of nature. Art asks artists to be honest, and to express to the world the greatness, the depths, and the generosity of our souls. Perhaps one of the great lessons for people, individually and collectively, is the use of power, and acts of art are microcosmic lessons in the use of power. Power generates, sustains, and destroys. In the lotus, power cracks the seed, urges the stem, flourishes as foliage, and generates the blossom and in art, power flows through the artist from idea to completed work. When we feel resistance, we know that life is asking us to join in the cycle of creation and to become powerful.

Power is used in many ways, to wage war, to foster peace, to create art, to wreak havoc, to love, to nurture, to control. Jaded by the overwhelming use and abuse of power that constantly surrounds us, we can be blind to the gentle expression of power that is conveyed through flower arranging. Flower arrangements carry with them the power to console, to bring joy, and to encourage. They enliven the atmosphere and add beauty. They dramatize events and soften life's more brutal moments. This is the power that flows through the flower arranger into the arrangement.

One day while delivering an arrangement in an office building, just as I was ready to step onto the elevator an elderly couple glimpsed the flowers and exclaimed, "How beautiful!" As we started a conversation, I set the arrangement on a nearby table so they could see it better. Then the gentleman looked into my eyes, as if peering directly into my soul, and said with a profound kindness, as though speaking for some disembodied angel, "you have made many people very happy!" I hoped in my heart, even as I knew in my soul, that he was right. This is a power worth living.

The next time you encounter resistance, see it as a vital step in the act of art. It is an invitation to pause and to prepare ourselves for the sacred act of creation, so that just as the stem of the lotus rises out of the water of the swamp, our acts of art emerge from our souls.

Chapter Eleven

Emotion

One day after a day off, I went into the flower shop where I was a part-time employee and looked at the display cooler, which was always supposed to have a certain number of arrangements in it. On this particular day it fell far short. I knew the load of playing catch up would fall on me and I became angry. Since there was at least an hour before another designer was scheduled to show up I decided to let the cooler situation rest and instead I chose to devote my time to designing my anger. With little premeditation, I selected a container and flowers and began to arrange. The arrangement included twigs, moss, Queen Anne's lace, spray roses, tulips, statice, heather, and daffodils in a low ceramic container. When completed, the arrangement carried the mood of a peaceful woodland, the antithesis of the emotion that motivated its creation. Through that act of art my anger was dissipated, I felt content, and I was able to carry on with my day, as I enjoyed my work and the camaraderie of my co-workers.

While creating that arrangement relieved my emotional stress, an act of art is not a quick fix to emotional discomfort; rather it is a channel for emotion. It would be tempting to explain how to use emotion, but emotion is not something to use, rather it is something to allow, to make room for. An awareness of emotion allows us to create from the depth of feeling.

A deep reservoir of soul, emotion, like water in the swamp, keeps the act of art moist and lively. Emotion can be still as a reflecting pool or rage with the fury of a stormy ocean. Amoral by nature, its power can be harnessed for good and ill alike. For the artist following the call of the soul, the currents of emotion carry the act of art.

There are two ways to consider the involvement of emotion in our acts of art, or any other aspect of life. One is when an act comes from emotion and the other is when it is performed with emotion. While the two seem similar and the differences seem subtle, there is the distance of a continent between them. When we act from emotion we serve it and it chooses the action. When we act with emotion we choose the action and emotion empowers the act. The former is an eruption and the latter is a flow and I have acted out of both. When acting from emotion I have stormed out of commitments and chased infatuations, and while acting with emotion I have created beautiful flower arrangements and written moving words.

While by nature emotion is often spontaneous, it is possible to deliberately tap into its reserve. I meet at least once with every bride before arranging her wedding flowers, but often I will meet two or more times. At a practical level the meetings are for decisions on colors, flowers and styles, however my underlying purpose is to become acquainted with the bride or the couple, if the groom is also available, so I will feel some emotional spark when I create the bouquets for their special day.

For instance I was meeting with a delightful young couple at their home for a second appointment just days before their wedding. They were struggling. The previous evening they had had dinner with family members who had been difficult and argumentative, plus emotions were running high, as often is the case, just because of the impending event. The flower order was small, a couple of bouquets, a few corsages and boutonnières, and one reception arrangement, but as I tell my brides, there may be small flower orders, but for the bride and groom there is no small wedding. Some weddings have simpler trappings, but the commitment and the moment is huge for them all.

That evening we talked for an extended period of time. I felt a great empathy for them, and was filled with admiration because of how seriously they were taking this commitment and how respectful they were of each other in their current conflict, and I felt sympathy for the unnecessary stress the family squabble placed on them. As I created the bride's bouquet, a free form cluster of pink roses, lavender lilacs, red tulips, pink wax flower, and cascading ivy, a bouquet compatible with the garden setting where vows were to be exchanged, I felt my care for the couple flow into it one flower at a time. Her bouquet not only sprouted with the blossoms of a spring garden, but with the joy and hope I felt for this couple who were already so actively engaged in the soul work of their partnership.

Emotion brings us into dialogue with our souls. Like the song of a bird, our souls sing through our emotions, affirming what is going well in our lives, and directing us to areas that need attention. When we are attentive to it, emotion facilitates the dialogue.

For instance, one Valentine's Day, while freelancing for another florist, I again worked long hours of high production. Just weeks before I had had one of the pinnacle experiences of my career and here I was once more, with my stamina running low, feeling depressed. I asked myself how could I go so high and fall so low in just a few short weeks. The days leading into the holiday were fun, but by this time I was feeling depleted. Then, as I made an arrangement, I felt directed to look at the flowers all around me and to see their colors. I was reminded that between white and black lies the rainbow and that life is a full-spectrum experience. That thought was the whisper of my soul. I was able to peacefully complete my Valentine's Day work, but also when the need for my work slowed, I took an early out to take care of myself.

Emotional well being is not about always being on an even keel, nor is it about controlling emotion, rather it is about recognizing emotion and its message, and allowing it a place in our lives. For artists it is about allowing emotion to fuel our art. When we do that, we are reaching the caverns beneath the rational mind where we find the reservoir of soul from which art springs, like a lotus from the swamp.

Chapter Twelve

Balance and the Center

Intermittently my life runs amuck, my finances hit the skid and I am again living the life of a starving artist. I learned long ago that it's a great story line for the opera but not much fun to live through. However I was born under the sign of Libra and perhaps my personal motto should be "feast or famine." I seem to always be living in the extreme. As one of my friends once said, Librans are born under the sign of the scales because they are always looking for balance, not because they have it.

Because of my Libra tendencies to imbalance, I've studied balance intently. Through observation, I've learned that balance is a welcome mat inviting one to enter and be comfortable. This is true in life and in flower arrangements alike.

Imbalance aggravates. When I visit a friend whose living room is arranged with all the heavy furniture at one end I feel driven to scurry about and rearrange it and when I see an arrangement that is out of balance, I am in a state of alert and I want to rescue it. Ultimately imbalance leads the eyes to reject the arrangement. On the other hand when an arrangement is in balance it encourages you to linger and soak up its pleasure.

Creating balance is an act of engagement. It engages the extremes of the arrangement in a relationship through the center that is comfortable for the eyes.

Symmetrical arrangements, where all the flowers are the same on both sides of the center, demonstrate this most clearly. The center is easily delineated and the equality of both sides makes this style of arrangement easy to look at, although its simplicity can verge on boring.

The more one veers from the simplicity of that style of arrangement the more stimulating the arrangement becomes visually and the more challenging it becomes to create. The first step beyond is still a symmetrical arrangement but where the flowers vary on each side. Beyond that is the asymmetrical arrangement with sides that are different in size but maintain balance with the weight of the color, variation in size of blossoms, or the counterbalance of other flowers outside the immediacy of the extremes.

Beyond symmetrical and asymmetrical, arrangements take many other forms, including round, oval, crescent, Hogarth curve (an S-shape arrangement), linear, and free form. While all of the arrangements differ from each other, those that are comfortable to the eye all have one thing in common: balance.

As the arrangement builds and all the other elements take their place, it becomes complex and exciting. Throughout the creation of the arrangement attention is still given to the relationship of the extremes.

Every flower has visual weight that comes from size, density, and color. This is easy to see if we contrast a football mum with a daisy, or a cateleya orchid with a sprig of baby's breath. When flowers play off of each other in an arrangement smaller flowers lighten heavier ones, which is, for instance, why baby's breath is so effective and popular with roses. In reverse heavy flowers give weight to lighter ones, which is why some heavier flowers are placed closer to the foundation of an arrangement.

Balance is established in the skeleton, but as an arrangement grows complex, balance is maintained through nuance: a branch in the shadows, a sunflower peeking out from behind a fern displaying only a few petals. Through nuance we add flesh to an arrangement, making it tender, even voluptuous, but in this simple dance each flower is playing off the other in a teeter-totter of balance that emanates from the center.

All arrangements must have a center; otherwise they are not arrangements at all but gathered chaos. The creation of a flower arrangement is the process of bringing order. To appreciate the difference between order and gathered chaos I only need to walk to my basement where the gathered chaos reigns supreme, bags of outgrown clothing tumble over boxes of books, next to opened plastic storage containers that overflow with odds and ends, and on and on. Everything landed where it landed, with no intent to order. Laziness not order guided their placement. But in one corner, I have a few carefully stored antiques, neatly placed. Order resides in that corner.

The center is the organizing element of the arrangement from which all the other elements radiate and where order and balance is established. In the craft of flower arranging the student learns to make the center a focal point -- the place where the eye comes to rest in an arrangement. In the art of flower arranging this may or may not be true. Many successful flower arrangements do not require focal points at all.

A complex arrangement may have more than one center. It is easy to conceptualize an arrangement with one center where all the flowers radiate from the focal point. Perhaps, however, it is more difficult to imagine an arrangement with multiple centers. One example that comes to mind is a European style made popular many years ago that still inspires many arrangements today.

Such an arrangement would consist of groupings of like vertical flowers all with parallel stems. So first several roses might be placed, each blossom appearing to sprout above the lower one. Then several liatrice, then snapdragons, followed by carnations placed in similar cadence to the roses. In an elongated container this arrangement could have many such groupings, all parallel, each sprouting from its own center, and yet all in harmony and balance, like a series of plants in a garden.

We can experience the importance of center if we pay attention to our bodies. We walk and stand from our centers, but we are not usually aware of it until we try to stand on one leg. When we do that we establish balance through our physical center.

Balance spins in and out of control each time another flower is placed. As the arrangement builds, it is grounded through the center. Finally when the last flower is placed, if the arrangement has sustained balance, it is comfortable to the eye.

There are few absolutes in flower arranging. Earlier I spoke of a must. All arrangements must have a center. Now I will give an absolute. Flower arranging is always about relationship, the relationship of the flowers to each other, and of the flowers to the container and of the flower arranger to the elements. Balance through the center is the means for the elements to relate to each other as compliments for the good of the whole.

Just as the stems and leaves of the lotus relate to its roots, making it stable in the swamp, center and balance create a stable arrangement that is comfortable to the eye and secure in its setting.

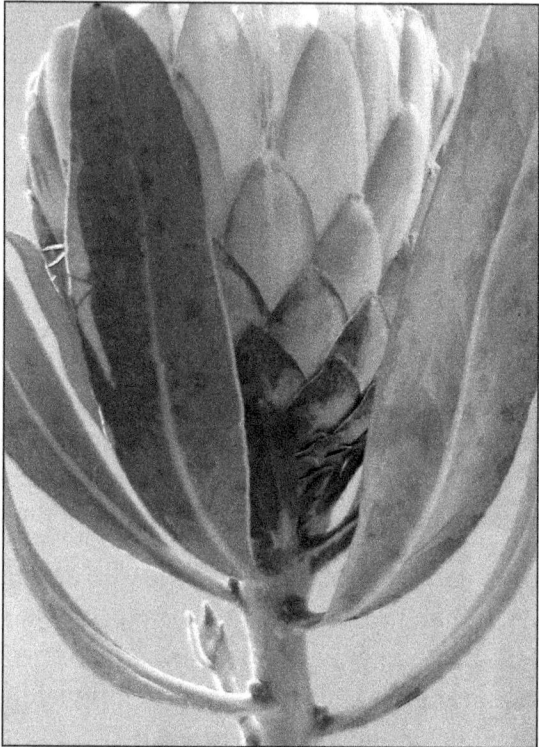

Protea

Chapter Thirteen

Struggle and Surrender

It is tempting to romanticize the act of art. For instance to imagine a painter in smock and beret, holding a paint palette as she stands in a bucolic field and paints trees, cows, and a pond. Or, in keeping with the theme of this book, to imagine a flower arranger standing at a table in a potting shed surrounded by the smell of humus tempered with the perfume of fresh cut roses as he happily makes an arrangement of flowers just picked from his garden. Every romantic vision holds some truth, but art seduces us to a deeper experience of soul than the romantic fantasy allows. It summons us to struggle and to surrender.

One evening I had a wedding appointment with a delightful and personable couple. Carrie, Paul, and I met at her mother's home and discussed their wedding plans and the flowers of their choosing. As with many couples I design for, Carrie and Paul were very trusting of my abilities, especially since two different people had referred me to them.

The appointment was going pleasantly enough with basic styles chosen and favorite flowers listed. Among their requests, they wanted to have center-pieces for each reception table. Their budget was ample for this and I was beginning to imagine simple, elegant arrangements with just a few flowers stylishly placed. These centerpieces would be more Ikebana styled than garden styled. This idea was inspired by both the conversation as well as the bride's gown. Carrie and Paul seemed pleased with my suggestions and were going to leave most of the details up to me.

Then just as I was about to leave, Carrie piped up, "I just love flowers. When our guests arrive at the reception I want them to see flowers!" The groom seconded the motion, and then just for a moment, in a few brief sentences, the two of them spilled over with how much they loved flowers, all kinds of flowers.

The arrangements I had in mind, while lovely, would not have expressed their deep love of flowers. For the next several weeks, as those final comments kept running through my mind, so did some incongruous ideas. I saw traditional center-pieces, vase arrangements, and Ikebana style arrangements, all of them begging for center stage. I was becoming very unsettled.

Then one day, while visiting the wholesale house, I saw some rather tall clear glass vases. I knew these were taller than what one usually uses for centerpieces because they would block the view of the guests across from each other. But I could not get them out of my mind.

Shortly thereafter, I met at the reception hall with Carrie and Paul. When I walked in I could see a pair of those vases filled with gladiolas, cymbidium orchid stems, alstromeria, roses, calla lilies, gerbera daisies, and cascading ivy, on two tables in the center of the hall. I realized it would be worth breaking the rules on a couple of tables to create the impact Carrie and Paul desired. The other tables would have lower arrangements, visually supporting the two taller vases. Altogether they would create the impression of lots of flowers that the bride and groom desired and would express their love of flowers.

Now the last debate was whether to use smaller companion vases for the rest of the tables or whether to go with traditional centerpieces. That debate lasted for many more days and had my stomach tied up in knots. Finally I called Carrie to see which she would prefer. She did not have a preference.

The internal debate ended when I went to the wholesale house and selected the companion vases. I simply made a choice. I then selected roses, alstromeria, and gerbera daisies, the same as in the large vases, along with green dendrobium orchids, mini calla lilies, liatrice, golden aster, and heather. In the end, Carrie and Paul were thrilled with their flowers. Carrie told me that it was as though I had picked pictures of what she wanted right out of her imagination.

When we struggle in the act of art we refine the outcome by picking and choosing, by accepting and releasing. Some ideas come to fruition, while others are released. Some flowers are chosen while others remain in the bucket or garden. One form is selected above all the others.

The great temptation in creative struggle is to give up. When we give up we make no decision and take no steps to fulfilling the potential of our creative idea. Instead we abandon the idea. My mother called this "throwing the baby out with the bath water."

Rather than giving up, engaging in an act of art requires surrender. When we surrender, we give in by taking action and by continuing in the process, even in the discomfort of the struggle and in the uncertainty of the outcome.

When I selected the vases for Carrie and Paul's wedding, I surrendered to one idea, one image for the centerpieces. Surrender guides the act of art and the placement of each flower in an arrangement is a reflection of that surrender. Through surrender we become engaged in the process and take action to move towards completion. When we surrender through the act of art, the arrangement is born, just as a lotus surrenders its bud to birth its blossom.

Chapter Fourteen

Pleasure, Grief, and Ecstasy

Like the fleece lining in leather gloves, pleasure is life's subtle plush and as with Annedore's Fine Chocolates, my hometown favorite, one taste invites the next. Pleasure invites us to life's banquet and seduces us to want more of all of life's bountiful goodness.

Indulging in pleasure is enjoying the conviviality of the Divine. Being an epicurean at heart, I have long believed the great gift of the loving Divine is to place us in a world ripe with pleasure, a world so delicious that it could serve as the model for the Garden of Eden. Also, I hold that one of the greatest ways we show our gratitude to that Divine is to indulge in those pleasures. Even in my own human way, when I have guests to my home, I know their gratitude when I see them enjoying what I have provided. No words of thanks substitute for the smiles on their faces and their good humor as they take pleasure in the conviviality of my table.

A love of pleasure also drew me to massage, where caring, intentional, disciplined touch relieves angst, relaxes body, mind, and soul, and places one in the disposition of accepting good feelings. After a massage I find myself singing more, walking more leisurely, and paying more attention to the subtle nuances of life.

In fact my philosophy of pleasure matured through the study of massage. As I gave massages, I noticed how others also relaxed into the comfort of pleasure, immersed in the natural sensations of their bodies. Many reported massage to be healing for body, mind, and soul.

What I have observed about massage is that the healing is in the pleasure. Just as a silver tray radiates its natural glow when the tarnish is removed, massages remove barriers to our enjoyment of life as tightened muscles, a stressed mind, and over worked emotions relax and allow natural good feelings to surface. People who seek to heal through many modalities of therapy, through bodywork, and in support groups are seeking to return to a natural good feeling.

We cannot, however, speak honestly of pleasure without speaking honestly of grief. There was a time in my life when the dark night of grief was so dense I thought I would never again see daylight. Friends died from AIDS and breast cancer. Heart attacks, car wrecks, and suicides claimed others. The elders of my family and community were dying from old age. Death decimated my community with such a rapid fire pace I could not catch my breath, nor did I want to. I, too, wanted to take my leave.

During those times, I began traveling to the mountains of Northern California for massage-based retreats, where the pain of grief mellowed as I allowed deep pleasure to touch body and soul. I still remember the first retreat after my mother's death as though it were only yesterday.

One day, while in a discussion with a small group of men, I shared the intensity and depth of my grief. Then Peter invited me to lie on the ground with my head in his lap. The others surrounded me and gently massaged my grief-tensed body. As Peter, a musician and composer, cradled my head, he chanted a Hebrew prayer. I was transported to pleasure's depths via their physical, spiritual, and soulful attention.

Moments of deep pleasure touch the very cells of our being and call them to reawaken to their natural good feeling. I remember walking through the woods after that massage feeling as though the majestic redwoods, noble firs, and live oaks were bowing to me like a maitre d' at a fine restaurant saying come to our feast and take your pleasure.

While oceans of tears purged my grief, it was the salve of deep pleasure that soothed my soul and awakened in me the will to live. To have its greatest impact, pleasure, like salve for skin, must be continuously applied.

We do not have to travel to some distant place or take in exotic experiences for pleasure to enter our lives and do its magic. In fact, too often we settle for so little in life when there is so much, and we do this because we are off chasing the grand, forgetting the truth of the old adage, "The best things in life are free." We are surrounded with opportunities for pleasure and the sense of well being that they can bring.

Their value underestimated, pleasures close at hand are often those most easily ignored. When we become aware of these blind spots, we can open our eyes and hearts and revel in simple indulgences. Flower arranging is filled with opportunities for pleasure, including all the obvious ones, but also many less obvious such as fluffing carnations.

Carnations shipped across the country from growers, often come to flower shops thirsty and shriveled from traveling days without water. Placed in warm water, about the temperature for a bath, with flower food they begin to wake up. However it can take two to four days for them to be fully open. So, as every florist knows, when the carnations have had some water and yet are still sleepy, we can help the carnations along by fluffing them with our hands. We take the blossom in one hand, and then cupping the other hand over the carnation, we gently smooth out the petals until the carnation is fluffy, fully awake. Of course this serves a practical purpose in having the carnation more readily available for an arrangement, but there is also a subtle pleasure in this act. The carnation against the palm of the hand tickles slightly, giving a pleasant sensation, a slight massage.

Too often pleasure is reserved for leisure time activities and then again those opportunities are too often devoured by seemingly more important activities. But pleasure, like a spring mist, touches all aspects of our lives and moistens even those most arid. Opportunities for indulging in pleasure are everywhere, taking a brief but leisurely walk on a break, burning incense or a scented candle while cleaning house, placing a flower on a desk.

Pleasure scattered throughout our lives is like baby's breath in an arrangement; it softens the deep colors and blends the elements. When an arrangement appears too heavy or too disunified some sprigs of babies breath will lighten the arrangement and bring it together.

Pleasure is the first delicate blossom of a greater ecstasy and when we approach the act of art with the intention of pleasure, we are entering slowly into our own ecstasy. Like a massage for the body, the act of art becomes a massage for the soul and ecstasy is one of the soul's natural good feelings. Of course not every act of art is an ecstatic experience, but as we continue to follow the call of our souls and to engage in acts of art, and as we allow pleasure to waft through these acts like incense in a room, we uncover soul's natural good feelings and know the ever-deepening levels of pleasure that eventually open to ecstasy, just as the lotus opens to the rising sun.

Chapter Fifteen

Shadow

A rt, like life, has its difficult moments. I often walk in the shadow of my art and am enmeshed in its mayhem like a dolphin in a fisherman's net. Happily making an arrangement, I can be saving one perfectly shaped, fluffy football mum for the focal point, and just as I am about to place it, the mum snags on a piece of greenery, shatters and all its petals fall. Then my Italian Irish blood pressure jumps over the roof. Or, just as an arrangement is about to be completed, the basket liner springs a leak and so I must dismantle the arrangement and begin again. A grimace on my face, and clenched teeth, warn me that shadow has plunged into my act of art.

Unlike serendipity, which I discuss in another chapter, shadow makes its presence known in difficulty and pain. It brings turmoil and uncertainty as it antagonistically challenges us to confront things not easily seen. Like a silent wasp on a screen, shadow waits. Opportunistically it plunges, disturbing the peaceful flow of art and life. What we find when we wrestle with shadow is unpredictable, as previously unknown strengths surface and stealth vulgarities show their ugly face. During shadow's visit we must trust soul's call and persevere. Then, when we rise to meet its challenges, however begrudgingly, we discover new depths in our souls.

I have often been ashamed and embarrassed by my mistakes, but worse, I have felt the same about my best. The antagonism of the shadow has led me to appreciate and respect my best and to accept the rest.

Perhaps my first experience in the shadow of art was an encounter with Sister Mary Juliana, my first grade teacher. Each first grader had a coloring book depicting the life of Jesus. One day in art class, as I was busily coloring away, Sister Mary Juliana leaned over my shoulder and screeched, "You're not coloring in the lines! You're not creative." Regardless of empirical evidence to the contrary, I ardently believed her message, which became an ingredient in the mud of my life, one I would deal with for many years as her message rang in my soul and became a personal mantra.

Sr. Mary Juliana's conclusion about me based on my coloring book set the stage for my struggle to identify myself as an artist. When she told me that I was not creative, she instilled in me the denial of my creative abilities, which became a recurrent theme in my life. Like the notes on a scratched record, it replayed again and again as I moved from flower shop to flower shop. Often, as I looked at the work of other arrangers I would lament that I was not a creative person. Of course I hid it well, exploding with accolades for their creativity as a mask for my own pain.

That self-doubt spawned by the shadow usurped much of my creative energy and frustrated my adventuresome spirit, as it led me to shun the practices and opportunities that could have enhanced my creative life. It also played into the hands of my immature ego, which was an overzealous friend and a subtle foe. Cheering me on to great accomplishments in my daydreams, my ego seldom credited the genuine accomplishments of my work nor registered the quality of my arrangements.

When provoked by shadow's agitation, my bohemian nature resented the monotonous monster of the daily discipline of the job. That monotony left me feeling as though my psychic energy was draining away into the throat of some cosmic vampire. While in the clutches of shadow's gloom, I called myself a flower whore. My well-being seemed to come second, at best, to making a buck by plying my trade.

When perturbed by shadow's restlessness, I became discontent with both flower arranging and my life. During those times, trapped in the shadow of my art, I wanted out! I sought other forms of artistic expression that I hoped would free me as I dreamt of the accomplished poetry I would some day write or the sculptures I would craft.

One day I stood in my own flower shop, despondent. I had battled the shadow's monsters for all they were worth and they seemed to be winning. I wondered why something I had so enjoyed pretending to do as a child had become such a nightmare in adult life.

The shadow can work as a stun gun and paralyze or it can be a great teacher. Standing there in my shop, I realized that I needed to decide which it would be and I chose the latter.

It took some time, but with the help of wise mentors, I chose to unburden myself of the overwhelming demands of a retail business and recreate my career. By doing this I was able to rejuvenate my passion for flower arranging.

As unwelcome as the shadow was at times, it was the voice that eventually drew me on in search of opportunities to further develop my talent. The cloudy days of my career caused me to look further into the soul of flower arranging as I sought salve for my wounded soul. Like an opponent on a battlefield, the shadow was the adversary that made me rise to meet the challenges of my art so that I could continue to reach for my creative potential.

It's impossible to predict when the shadow will rear its ugly little head, when it will send us into a tailspin, or when we will encounter a deeper knowledge of ourselves and our art from its presence. There was a time when I made an arrangement every Sunday for a little church in South Kansas City. I also decorated their sanctuary for Christmas and Easter. Their holiday budget was always ample, but while they paid me more than my cost, I contributed by charging well below market value. Also, for some of those holidays, a team of volunteers helped to install the work. This one particular year was no exception. We gathered on a Saturday morning to install the Christmas arrangements and the work went off without a hitch. I was pleased and the volunteers loved the finished design.

The next day I went to the service and was flabbergasted. Everything was rearranged and partially dismantled. It looked horrible. Minutes before the service I was loudly vocal to the church officials about my displeasure. They, in turn, informed me that they had in effect purchased the arrangements and that they could do as they pleased with them. It struck me in the core of my being: to them they were merely decorations; to me they were my art. I shouted to Sister Mary Juliana, and to every cell in my being, that indeed I was creative! And that I was an artist and that those arrangements were my art. All the compliments of my career had not elicited that guttural response. It took the shadow to affirm my art.

It is natural to want to escape the shadow's difficulties by discarding an errant arrangement or walking away from our art. But sooner or later, like storm clouds blown away by the wind, the shadow will leave. As we meet the challenges and resolve the difficulties presented by shadow, we strengthen our artistic resolve, expand our creative abilities, and come to know the mettle of which we are made.

Ginger

Chapter Sixteen

Rhythm, Layers, and Texture

While driving I love to take note of the rhythms of nature. The motion transforms the landscape into a visual symphony. I count the rhythm of the trees I pass. I am aware that some trees are given their beat for human purpose such as the tall slender evenly spaced poplars planted by the farmers for windbreaks. The rest beat to nature's drum, springing up to her count.

I count a cluster of four pines, space, a maple, space, a thunderous oak, space, two more pines, space, and then six tall plump cedars beating a staccato. Their quick beat brings me to attention. Many trees that I do not know by name enter and take up the rhythms. Small shrubs make their entrance as well. Nature's whisper is almost audible as she directs their entry, "Pianissimo, Pianissimo," "Soft, soft," as she maintains her rhythms.

I become aware of the layers. Behind the row where I have been keeping time stands trees, rocks, shrubs and ponds which contribute to this visual symphony. They counterbalance the melody and give incredible depth to the performance. At times the elements of those layers beat in tandem and at other times they titillate with syncopation. A legato begins and all the elements in the layers become one long smoothly flowing phrase. They are not a whole note being held through many measures, but clusters, and individuals gliding flawlessly one into another. Like entwined branches their connection to each other gives continuity. Regardless of the particulars from one movement to the next, each is a flawless performance orchestrated by nature.

Add to the rhythms the colors and textures, and I am awash in the music. My artist soul takes note of the exquisite subtleties that make up the performance.

Rhythm connects the individual components of a composition, allowing each note its own identity and place in the music. Varying rhythms add interest to a composition without which all music would be one endless line of equal notes.

The rhythm that surrounds us is sometimes composed of spontaneous beats, like the trees, shrubs and rocks lining my drive. At other times it can be the boring pace of a row of suburban houses all the same color and design, and at still other times it is the varied rhythms of a symphony. Music uses measured intentional rhythm while nature is more spontaneous, but both rhythms engage the audience and entice them to listen to the music.

We too have our rhythms. I remember being at the doctor's for an echocardiogram. I lay on my side watching the monitor that showed the beat of my heart. Then the doctor turned on the sound and I heard a rhythmic slush. "My rhythm!" I exclaimed to myself.

I often think about the pace and rhythms of my life. I am one who, as the cliché goes, often walks to the beat of a different drum. I meander about my life lazily, almost a slow legato of motion, and then something strikes my fancy or demands a hurried attention and I am off and running, doubling or even tripling my pace. At times I become a living staccato as I start, stop and start and stop.

I love participating in drumming circles and I attend nearly anytime I am invited. I was hesitant and awkward at the first ones because I felt out of sync with everyone else. Eventually I began hearing all the varied beats that were making the majestic sound. Rhythm is seductive. As I listened to the beats of the others I could not resist entering the circle with my own.

Flower arrangements, too, need rhythm to be seductive. I first began arranging flowers when nosegays were coming into vogue. In the ultimate nosegay, every single flower stood even with the next, until a perfect ball was created, sometimes so perfect you could nearly bounce them. We were admonished at those demonstrations to let every flower stand up and be counted. After all, we were told, our customers were paying for every flower, so they should be able to see each one.

In those pristine nosegays, there was little room for the flourishes of rhythm. Like music with only quarter notes in four-four time, such an arrangement holds little interest beyond the first glance. People became quickly bored with that style of nosegay since our eyes and souls need something more rhythmic if they are to linger with the arrangement.

In music, rhythm defines the relationship of the notes and decides the attention each note will receive. An eighth note measures half a quarter note, which measures half a half note, which measures half a whole note. A fleeting eighth note alone gets little notice, while a whole note by comparison hogs the stage. However, place a run of eighth notes together and their pithy presence enlivens the musical composition. The vitality of a musical composition rests in the mix of the various notes.

In the same way, visual rhythm brings an arrangement to life. Take for instance the humble boring nosegay. To add spice to this most traditional of flower arrangements, we need only to cluster some flowers, perhaps a few daisies, allow some freesia to prance staccato through the arrangement, place some flowers in pairs and others as triplets. A proud rose alone here and there throughout the arrangement will add drama like an extended whole note. Placing some flowers deeper towards the center and others on the surface of the plane builds the layers and now the boring nosegay has become enchanting.

A well-crafted arrangement that becomes a work of art depends on the subtleties of its layers, not the perfect layers of a birthday cake, rather the interwoven layers of nature. The layers of an arrangement hold the subtlety of the details and, as we move through the arrangement, we create the subtlety as we continue to layer in the flowers, greens and other elements. Some stand in the forefront, while others take a back seat, and still others become so lost in the shadows they are barely visible, but they too are making their contribution.

In those layers the different elements beat to varying rhythms and weave themselves together, creating complex textures – soft, prickly, velvety, sharp edged. Most of us respond quickly and intuitively to texture, being either easily repulsed or seduced by it. I, for example, am warmed by the ripples of a chenille throw and repelled by the prickle of a cactus. Each flower possesses luscious textures, whether velvet or sandpaper. I love the texture of flowers, foliage, mosses and branches as an arrangement becomes a tapestry of textures.

The strength of an arrangement, like a symphony, lies in the subtlety of its details as rhythms beat and textures flow in its layers. Now the arrangement explodes with individual personality and seductive quality.

The complexity of the arrangement seduces the eye to linger and enjoy the beauty. Such complexity is not dependent on the quantity of elements, but on the imaginative use of them. A flower arrangement begs to be enjoyed when, beyond its surface beauty, its layers hold the magic of exquisite subtleties. Such an arrangement encapsulates the beauty of nature and celebrates the exuberance of the earth.

Chapter Seventeen

Color and Seeing

I am fortunate to live in an area that experiences the drama of four distinct seasons. Occasionally I consider leaving the Midwest and moving to some place with little summer or little winter, but I know I would miss the allure of the color of the seasons. They each hold their own romance and majesty.

The world is filled with delicious colors that invigorate the soul. When it comes to color, nature has been my best teacher and mentor and most inspiring muse, and it is her audacity with color that I want dancing throughout my arrangements.

I was born in September. Perhaps that fact explains the great delight I take in the magnificent colors of nature's autumn tapestry. My spirits soar as I note even the slightest change in the leaves as they begin their transformation from forest green. I love the burgundy of oak leaves, and the maple's vibrant red, or the orange of bittersweet, the tan of cornstalks, and the deep brown of acorns. I want to wrap myself in the warmth of these colors as I prepare to settle in for winter.

But then I also revel in the colors Mother Nature dresses herself in as she bursts into spring. My heart dances with her as I see again the dainty purple crocus or the sun drop yellow daffodils. As spring is birthed and the earth is robed again in the rainbow, lilacs, roses, forsythia, red bud, iris, and dandelions gush forth with their color. Each color enters and takes its bow as it awakens from winter's sleep, and I also am re-awakened.

Winter, too, holds my attention because during this season when there is less flamboyant color, I see the exquisite subtleties of nature's bones in the richness of the barren tree branches. I see the dusty brown of the sleeping grass and the dark, nearly black, green of the frozen ivy. When she chooses a mantle of snow, I love the combination of the white snow and vivid blue sky, as they fashion a fairy tale atmosphere against the muted and sleepy colors of Mother Nature's nightgown as she takes her winter's rest.

I love no less the intensity of summer's masquerade when the earth becomes a mirror reflecting back to the sun his intense radiance. As I look at the sunflower's gold, or the coneflowers deep purple, the sage's dusty blue, or the celosia's magenta, I nearly feel a slight burn as though the sun himself has touched my skin.

Like many flower arrangers, I learned about color combinations from the use of the color wheel. I was first introduced to this instrument in a high school art fundamentals class where we took the primary colors, red, blue, and yellow, plus white, and made charts with seventy-two colors. I was enthralled as the colors blended before my eyes. Then in flower school we worked with the color wheel as an aid in flower arranging. While the charts are helpful at times, such a cerebral approach to color is difficult for me to grasp. Oh, but in nature!!!

In nature each season has its distinct palette. I imagine Mother Nature standing before the mirror in her dressing room as she works with her frocks and changes from season to season. Those are the colors that communicate with my soul. And what I see is that the same colors flow from season to season, but their placement and intensity change. The colors that dressed the flowers in summer are now vividly present in the leaves of autumn. The colors of spring that were so light and airy become intense in the summer. The yellow that paraded through the jonquils in the spring becomes the gold in summer's sunflowers, and the amber in autumn's leaves and the umber in the winter remains of a harvested field.

When I go to nature for inspiration, the mundane becomes magical and the ordinary pulses with vitality. Often I have kicked a rock thinking it was nothing, but on closer examination it is a marvelous free form sculpture, with its shape and texture chiseled by millennia of existence.

As I follow nature's lead, fallen leaves in late autumn inspire an arrangement that captures the rich golden hues blended with a certain bleak emptiness. Those leaves that were high on the branches now rest on the ground, the lush green canopy now lies there, an amber blanket. However, beneath the leaves the green grass still peaks out and the many plants still maintain their leaves until winter's freeze.

I will begin my autumn arrangement with a dense layer of leather leaf, which reminds me of the rich forest ferns. Then, like the ground, I will cover that with a layer of autumn leaves. To echo the now-barren branches of the trees, I will place leafless branches radiating from the center. Bittersweet vining throughout the branches will complete the arrangement, which now speaks eloquently of the transitional nature of autumn as the earth moves from lush summer to sleepy winter.

Nature overflows with instruction. Her lessons come as we sit with her beauty and become the proverbial sponge soaking up her instruction and her inspiration. As we sit absorbing her lessons, we learn best if we look with soft eyes. Whether in a park, a garden, a field, a forest, by a river, in the mountains or on the plains, lessons occur anywhere we become reflective and receptive. Often as we hurry about our days we look without seeing, but when we sit with Mother Nature and view her with soft eyes, we begin to see differently, more fully.

Looking with soft eyes is nearly like squinting, but not at all tense; it is sleepy eyed yet totally aware. At this point our critical eye will go for a well-deserved rest. The critical eye is important because it deconstructs and allows us to see details. Effectively used it delineates those details and points out strengths and weaknesses for the purpose of improvement. But the critical eye can become a petty tyrant if allowed too much importance. With it in command nothing is ever good enough and everything is a stretch to unattainable perfection.

Soft eyes perceive the nuances of beauty and see with the tenderness of the heart like a lover gazing at his beloved. We live in a delicious world composed of sensuous, fluid layers, which, like waves, flow one into the other. When looking with soft eyes we see the layers and sense their flow, we see the whole rather than fragments, the composition rather than just the individual stems. Soft-eye viewing allows us to see the marriage between solids and space and to explore dimension.

Soft eyes guide our journey inward where we behold beauty and experience the pleasure of nature's seasonal palettes. These palettes are the celebration of moods through the many shades and tones of the rainbow. By looking at nature through soft eyes, we bathe our souls in her colors and dress our hearts in her frock and as floral artists we weave her tapestry through our arrangements.

The experience of creating art deliteralizes life. The meteorologist knows the speed of the wind but artists hear its melody; the technician depends on a color wheel, but an artist draws on the inspiration of nature's tapestry. As artists, we know dimensions not seen and give birth to expressions before unspoken. This is our foray into the mystical where we touch the sacred.

Chapter Eighteen

Serendipity

My fondest memories of holidays when I was a boy are those of Easter. Christmas was often opulent, even during our family's financially disastrous times, because Santa Claus and the extended family regaled me with gifts. But it was the Easter Bunny's simplicity that won my heart. Each Easter, I received a basket covered with cellophane, tied with pretty ribbons. Inside were my favorite candies on a bed of grass and hidden beneath was a small gift. I loved looking at my Easter basket, just as I now love to look at a flower arrangement. Even after I opened it to dig for candy, I would retie the cellophane with the ribbon so I could continue to enjoy its colorful delight.

Now with most of those gifts forgotten, I still remember the hours I spent savoring the baskets and their treasures. However, some gifts I do remember. One year I received a stapler and staples. Then as now my desktop was barely visible. Excited to have that gift, I cleaned my entire desk, inside and out, determined to find its perfect home. I still have and use that stapler.

In some ways I haven't changed so much. Inspired by a new trinket that was either a gift or a find when junking, I will clean and rearrange an entire room until I find just the right place for it. There is no shortcut here, since once something is absorbed into the tapestry of my home, the pleasure of its newness quickly fades. As with the presents from the good bunny and gifts and serendipitous finds during a treasure hunt, I often find myself rearranging my life to make room for other unexpected visitations. An impromptu dinner invitation or a last-minute flower order will spur me to reorganize my calendar. A new friend interrupts the flow of my normal social life. Like the fun little gifts from the Easter Bunny, I love these happy surprises, the serendipity.

Serendipity provides the opportunity to flex the creative muscle spontaneously. On one such occasion I was about to decorate a wedding cake. The wedding was booked through a bridal consultant with whom I worked regularly. As she was putting the finishing touches on the buffet table, I approached the monster cake. Like twin towers, parallel cakes on plastic pillars rose from two sheet cakes with plastic stairs bridging the round tiers. There was a lot of cake!

As I walked over to it, I realized one tower was about to topple. "Gloria!" I screamed as I caught the cake. Gloria sped over. Between the two of us, we did the best we could to set it back up and to stabilize it. However there was damage. The caterer had already left and taken with her any extra cake icing that might have proven handy in attempting repair. Fortunately I had plenty of extra flowers, so I began my floral work. Where there had been chunks of cake before, clusters of ivy, with little pink sweetheart roses, white daisies, lavender wax flower and babies breath now sprouted. Because I was able to flower over most of the damage, the cake was lovely. However, it was a stroke of good fortune that I had not touched the cake before it toppled, and that, for the couple's sake, I had the skill to bring a creative touch to the unexpected.

I must confess, I enjoyed rescuing the wedding cake and the cake became something it would have never been had it not begun to topple.

Not all moments of serendipity are as grand as a collapsing wedding cake; some are so subtle they can be easily missed. For instance serendipity may present itself in the curve of a stem, or tilt of a blossom, or the shade of the flower. It may present itself in the way two flowers unexpectedly blend together or it can be at work when two flowers hold such a contrast that they appear to fight each other.

Presenting an opportunity for spontaneity, serendipity pushes the edge of the imagination one step further than was predetermined. We can plan an arrangement; we see it complete in our mind's eye; then diligently follow that plan. Suddenly in a serendipitous moment, we are off and running with a whole new direction and our act of art is gushing with fresh expression.

Art, like the lotus knows no bounds for offering its joy. The act of art is possessed by an adventure-some spirit and when the serendipitous moment is seized we are fully in the fun of the act of creation. When we realize the full breadth and depth of the joy of the creative act, we realize that we have tapped into the place of soul where fun again en-tices us to be children at play.

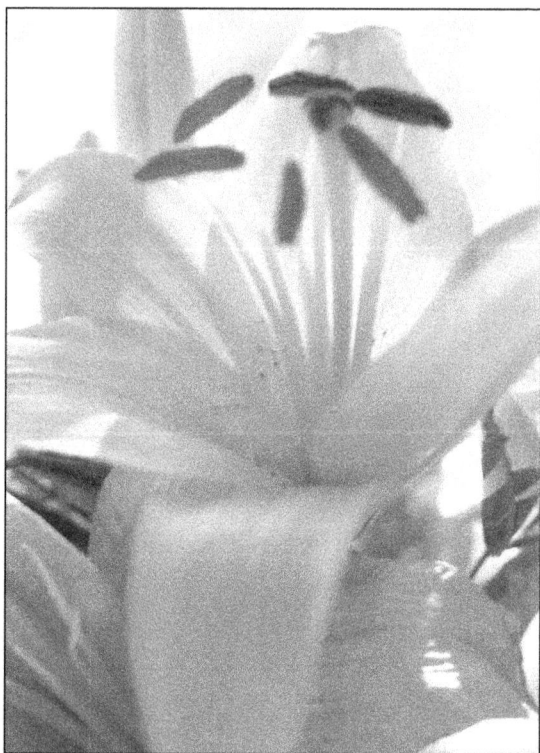

Lily

Chapter Nineteen

Sacred Places

There is a mystery beyond me, a mystery from which I was born and to which, one day, I will return. This mystery holds everything, art and science, the beautiful and the ugly, the lion and the sparrow, the calla lily and the dandelion. One of the wonders of this life is that we can reach to and touch that mystery. While there are many ways to do this, one way to reach is through creativity, one way to touch is through flowers. Sacred places remind me to reach and to touch.

My entire life has been a pilgrimage to the sacred. Even in the most mundane and profane times, I have sought the holy and the beautiful in the company of flowers. As well, I have been drawn to sacred places where my soul absorbed the beauty and bathed in a sense of the holy. As a boy, I frequently visited our parish church where flowers often adorned the altar. There my love of flowers became entwined with my love of the sacred.

I was fortunate to be raised Catholic in the pre–Vatican II era. It was a time when spirituality and beauty were the essence of the building and the ritual. St. James Church, our home parish, was a place where I experienced both and where I cultivated my love for flowers. The altar was a masterpiece carved as a single unit in Carrara, Italy. Its trim looked like stalagmites. Angels carved from the same marble stood with torches on each side. High above was a carving of a weeping Madonna holding her slain son carved in the style of Michelangelo's Pieta. During special times such as Easter and Christmas, flowers banked the altar. They were entwined between the twelve ornate brass candlesticks that stood three up and three down on either side of the tabernacle. I frequently visited the church just so I could take in the glorious array of flowers that were displayed against that regal backdrop.

My first remembered moments of awe were at St. James during Solemn High Masses on Christmas Eve and the Easter Vigil, where the spicy aroma of incense, the joyous organ music, the ethereal Gregorian chant, the cascades of flowers, and the reverence of the congregation all made a glorious blend that transported me to near ecstasy.

In the mid sixties, during my preteen years, the Second Vatican Council mandated changes in the liturgy that included using an altar that faced the congregation. The hierarchy at St. James seized the moment to modernize the sanctuary. They hired a crew to chisel the high altar into a pile of ruble. I still have a paperweight-size fragment of the altar. After the high altar had been destroyed to make way for contemporary liturgy, the sanctuary was less stirring, but still I found inspiration there for both my love of the sacred and my love for flowers. In fact early in my career I went to work for Silver Flower Shop, the very shop that had provided the flowers that I had admired at St James for all those years. I felt a thrill as I stood at the design table and realized I was now the one creating those displays.

Following my passion for spirituality, I have visited many sacred places where I stood in awe as I viewed the contributions of other artists that were so clearly born from their souls. Through these visits, I came to a deeper understanding of the soul of flower arranging and its relationship to the community.

At both great cathedrals and simple chapels I paused at the gargoyle fashioned by the stonemason or the saint hewn from marble by the sculptor or the vessels fashioned by the potter. I saw their compelling contributions encouraging the visitor to stop and enjoy a moment of awe.

By seeing the effect of these works of art, I came to understand that when flowers are brought to the altar they are not just added garnish, but they too help to create a place for an experience of the sacred, a moment of awe. They say to people who happen in, "Take note! This is an important moment." As I met the sacred through the works of other artists, I knew that I too was led by soul to share the sacred with others through flower arrangements.

Today, I do not limit my definition of sacred space to churches, mosques, synagogues, temples, or shrines. I consider any place that reminds us to reach to and to touch the mystery a sacred space. In my role as a floral artist it is my intention to create flower arrangements that will enhance the beauty and the soul of those places wherever they are.

My understanding of the soul of my work deepened as I visited churches and cathedrals, but it expanded as I appreciated soul for its ability to be present at any moment and in any place.

Just as the lotus needs a swamp, our relationship with the sacred needs places that nourish. When we invite the qualities of soul into a place, whether that place is a home, a garden, an office, a hospital room, or a restaurant, that place becomes holy ground where the sacred, spoken or silent, is present and known.

Chapter Twenty

Space

About 50 miles east of Kansas City are the beautiful Powell Gardens where I often spend hours enjoying the beauty of nature as it is arranged through the gardener's art. I walk the gardens slowly, as I gaze at the different plants that are displaying their delicious blooms. In the spring I especially enjoy going to their woodland garden where a brook cascades through the splendid azaleas that sprinkle the waking woodlands with color. There in the midst of the water and the azaleas I become spellbound. In July I revel in the perennials. The day lilies blaze among coneflowers, liatrice, shrub roses, Russian sage, bee balm, and verbena. On my walks through the garden I take advantage of the frequent benches where I sit and luxuriate in the beauty.

In a garden, art is experienced more fully than through any other medium as all the senses become engaged. The garden regales vision; its fragrances intoxicate and its textures, when one dares to touch, tickle the fingers; insects and birds serenade with their music. When I am in a garden my imagination meanders lazily and my soul drinks deep.

While there, I am not only aware of the flowers and trees that have been meticulously planted or the grass that is so carefully tended, or the water that mesmerizes, I am also aware of the sky dancing above and weaving itself between the trees and amid the stems. A ribbon that binds the elements of the garden together, it encases the rocks and marries itself to the ponds. Space in an arrangement is like the sky in a garden. It dances among the flowers and ties them together.

The unifying presence of space in a garden or an arrangement often goes unnoticed because our eyes have been lazy, as they look easily at the solids and ignore the space. As we become adept at seeing space our view of the world changes and we see our surroundings more intimately.

This ability to see space as well as the mass of an object allows us to know the complex whole, and makes the world and its objects more interesting. When space is ignored, everything appears flat but when it is included we are entertained by depth, dimension, and subtle detail.

The ability to perceive space is essential to the art of flower arranging, where the same characteristics of depth, dimension, and subtle details must be present. When space is consciously incorporated as an essential element in an arrangement, the arrangement becomes a little world all of its own.

Space is a pocket of emptiness that allows us to glimpse into the depths of our arrangements. As we place flowers deep, near the foundation, and then slightly above those, and then to the surface, layers are created. But for those layers to be enjoyed, space must be left in the arrangement to allow one to peer into its depths. There we find that the sweetheart rose or daffodil that appears to be sunk and lost actually has meaning in the arrangement.

Leaving space is a difficult discipline to practice. Anyone can clump flowers together but it takes an artist to master the relationship and the flow between what is there and what is not and to make meaningful their relationship. I've seen more than one flower arranger create lovely arrangements and then ruin them by going back through and "filling in all the holes."

To relax into the discipline of leaving space, we need to become comfortable with emptiness. Too often we pack our shelves, our closets, our rooms, and our schedules with "stuff" just to avoid emptiness. Too often, our lives become filled with junk because we feel anything is better than nothing. But our souls love to sit in the emptiness.

In the emptiness lies all memory and all possibility just as an empty container recalls an arrangement I once made and suggests another one that I might someday make. Emptiness is not merely the absence of something, it is also the possibility of something, and in emptiness we can dream of both.

As well, emptiness allows us to see into our depths. To appreciate this we only have to look at a window and see how its emptiness allows us to look to the depths of the world beyond its pane.

As winter is to spring, emptiness is to life and space is to an arrangement. The absence makes meaningful the presence. When we weave space through an arrangement we can remember that all emptiness and all presence dance together in a continual relationship of birth and death and that just as the lotus is absent in the winter it will again sprout in the spring and bloom in the summer. We do not need to be afraid of space, but rather to celebrate the exquisite opportunity it allows us to enjoy the depths not only of our arrangements but of our lives.

Chapter Twenty-one

Eros and Intimacy

W hen we give ourselves over completely to the act of art, as we draw from the depths of our souls, we come to a moment of sublime surrender. This is the journey of intimacy, and Eros becomes our guide as we are seduced to take the path.

His seduction begs my curiosity as a need to follow his bidding wells my gut, pulses in the caverns of my soul and explodes in the cells of my body. Eros, the tempter, dances through my life spewing invitations, and I welcome him, and I am invigorated by his seduction. He plays on my deep longings to connect and commune and he teases my yearnings to feel whole and complete. He promises that in his mystery lies union. His invitation evokes an innate desire deep within my soul to take my place in the wholeness of life. Eros disrupts the monotony of the mundane, exciting me with anticipation of the greatest pleasure and the closest intimacy.

When I try to ignore him, Eros becomes a constant beggar beast, leaving me no peace. I sometimes think Eros would have me enslaved to him, but through my acts of art I find instead that he has invited me to participate as an equal and that his invitation energizes me. In this way my acts of art are not the impotent gestures of a eunuch attempting to stave off a beast, they are a contest with Eros himself where intimacy is won.

When I begin an act of art, I feel the presence of Eros. As I place the first flower, and then the next, I feel myself responding to his invitation. I am along for the trip, a full body, full-being trip. A completed flower arrangement is not the destination of this journey. The destination is an act of art that comes from the depth of soul.

I became acquainted with Eros and his demanding invitations in sex. Then I learned that sex itself was not the destination intended by Eros' invitation, it was only one avenue. The destination is intimacy. Sex and art are two of the ways that Eros becomes physical, but at soul level Eros is about intimacy and intimacy is about knowing: knowing oneself, knowing others and knowing life itself. And it is about being known.

Intimacy's knowledge is experiential, not intellectual. It is the experience of the lotus when its roots are massaged by the mud, or its stem when pressed by the breeze, or its leaves and petals when warmed by the sun or moistened by the rain. It is the experience of the body held with a passionate embrace, of the heart filled with joy by love, or broken by grief, or the soul overflowing with fulfillment. Eros brings an equal fullness to acts of sex and acts of art alike.

Every time we pick up a flower with the intention of engaging in an act of art we are being drawn into an intimate experience. As we relish its beauty, respect its individuality, place it in relationship to other flowers, we are following Eros. As we move deeper into the experience, pacing the flowers rhythmically, blending their colors, drawing lines and defining form with them, we are dancing with Eros. In the moment of surrender, the imagination, the creative act, and the flowers together flow through us and this is the state of sublime surrender.

I have become an enthusiastic follower of Eros as he continues to bid me to follow him on this journey of knowing. In the end, after I have dissected, categorized, theorized, and philosophized about Eros, sex, and art, there is the act of arranging flowers, and making a flower arrangement is one of the ways that I make love in the world.

As we journey with Eros we come to our deepest realms. We are not there on a fact-finding mission. Nor are we getting more information about our relationships, or our likes and dislikes. We are not learning more about how to do our jobs, or what is the right food for our bodies. We are experiencing ourselves, our goodness, and our truth and as well we are experiencing the goodness and the truth of life. This is the journey of intimacy. When we accept Eros' invitation we shed the comfortable cocoon of the bud, we are instead the lotus coming into bloom.

Chapter Twenty-two

Scale

I feel privileged any time I am invited to arrange flowers for a special moment or a special place, but one invitation stands above all the rest. Each January in Omaha, Nebraska, the people of Saint Cecilia's Cathedral hold their Cathedral Flower Festival. Flower arrangers from the area bring their flowers and create gorgeous displays in different areas of the Cathedral. For an entire weekend the Cathedral glows with the presence of the magnificent array of flowers.

In January 1993, my friend Fritz Bally called and told me that I was to suit up and show up for that year's festival. He was creating the master plan for the arrangements for the sanctuary and he wanted me to co-design. Fritz was a prince of a man. Besides being a top floral designer, he was a painter. He had studied at the Kansas City Art Institute. While in New York earning his livelihood from flowers, he was a contemporary and friend of Andy Warhol. For personal reasons, he had moved to Omaha after an HIV diagnosis. At the time of the Cathedral Flower Festival he was coming to terms with the life he had lived and the potential for an early death, all the while intending a very long life. During his time in Omaha, Fritz completed an entire portfolio of paintings that dealt with his life and his relationships. One evening during my week with Fritz, he displayed all those paintings and shared with me stories about the people, events, and emotions that had inspired them. Listening to his life story while viewing those paintings was indeed one of the most intimate and treasured moments of my life. As I experienced their power I came to know his soul more deeply, and I came to appreciate the source of all his beautiful, moving, and powerful work. After all to see an artist's work is to glimpse his or her soul.

In his work, as in almost everything he did, Fritz brought an intensity that could electrify. So I was not shocked when he laid before me his plans for the sanctuary. We would work with only two colors, red and yellow, and there would be lots of both. Fritz decided that the entire sanctuary would glow with red carnations and forsythia. Fritz did the arrangements for the high altar. At its peak, just below the crucifix and above the tabernacle, he arranged a large bouffant of forsythia, an amount that required the harvest of many bushes. From the forsythia, hundreds of red carnations cascaded down each side of the tabernacle. Meanwhile I arranged large, freestanding pieces to scatter throughout the sanctuary. Each was made either entirely of carnations or forsythia. Fritz also asked me to arrange forsythia above the Bishop's chair.

Trouble! The freestanding arrangements went great, but the chair got me. I was not used to arranging flowers for the scale of that cathedral, so while Fritz was creating a bouffant of forsythia that shouted all the way to the back of the Cathedral, my arrangement over the bishop's chair barely whispered to the front pew. Fritz laughed and told me, "more, more!!!!" And I stuck in a few more branches. Finally he climbed down from his work on the high altar and came and stood by me and said, "No, like this!" as he stretched out his arms to show the wide expanse of forsythia he wanted me to use. Finally I got it! Fritz truly understood the grand scale of that cathedral.

My conflict with Fritz's instructions resolved itself when I thought, "scale!" I realized that the arrangement was fine, only it needed to be several times larger. Then I was able to complete my work to Fritz's satisfaction.

By the time we completed our work in the sanctuary we used approximately two thousand red carnations and bunches and bunches and bunches of forsythia. The effect was bombastic. Throughout the weekend Fritz and I returned time and again to watch the impact on people as they walked through the cathedral and also to admire and enjoy the work of the other floral artists, whose arrangements were equally stunning.

That week in Omaha was one of the highlights of my creative life. I savor the memories of those intimate conversations with Fritz and the joy of being lead through his artwork; the opportunity to work with him and be mentored by him; the opportunity to see the work of other floral artists in that sacred space; and the pleasure of the camaraderie of the good people of the Cathedral who hosted the festival.

As memorable as that moment in my life was, and as deeply satisfying and fulfilling, I find the same satisfaction and fulfillment in creating a small woodland arrangement, or a spring garden basket, or a tropical arrangement with some bamboo, a couple of birds of paradise and a cymbidium orchid...satisfied and fulfilled ...to scale that is! And in those moments, I know the lotus in bloom.

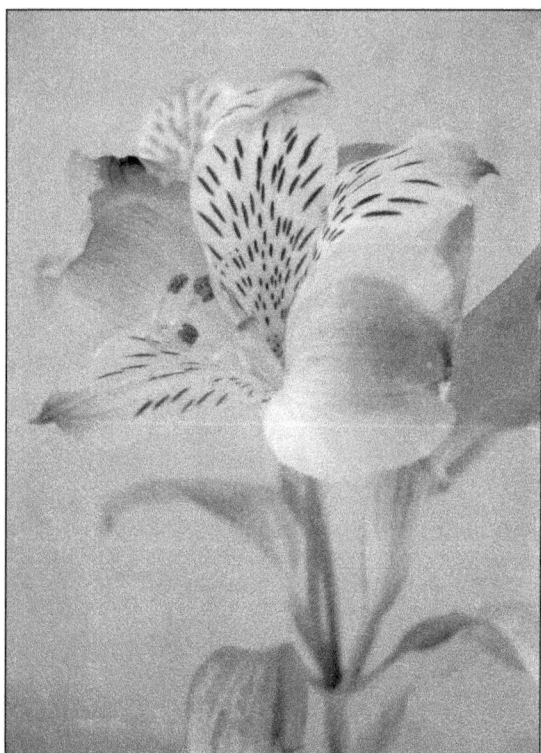

Alstromeria

Chapter Twenty-three

Artist Soul

A lotus grows from seed to blossom almost imperceptibly, yet its progress is evident. As we follow soul, we too may make progress nearly imperceptibly because soul travels its meandering way at is own pace, uninspired by the clock, or the drive for success, or a rush to accomplish. Soul is as likely to step back into memory, pause for reflection, and dream through dark nights, as it is to inch forward for progress. Still as it goes its own way it blossoms with a full body bouquet. As we follow its call, we walk with soul on this meandering path.

True to the desires and preferences of my soul, I have lived my life in Bohemian style, a vagabond following the calls of my soul. Along the way I questioned the road and the road signs. I spent long periods of time lost. Sometimes I reveled only in the journey and did not care a tinker's damn about the destination. I gazed at the stars and I danced naked in the moonlight. I dined at banquets fit for a king, and I picnicked in out-of-the-way places; sometimes I felt the pangs of hunger and could not find food. Often I traveled alone and at other times my trip was filled with exciting and interesting fellow travelers.

Along the way people often asked me who I am. I gave a legion of answers, names and titles that coincided with my enthusiasms, passions, struggles or relationships at the moment: son, husband, brother, lover, designer, artist, bohemian, student, poet, worker, teacher, etc. But beneath any name, like roots beneath the ground, there is one reality from which all the names spring--soul. Like a tuning fork in the tuner's hand soul confirmed when the name was right. I heard the discord when it was wrong because when we listen to soul we come to know ourselves, our depths and our heights.

I know my soul as certainly as I know my right hand. I see its reflection in a flower: soft, fragrant, colorful like the blossom; sturdy but pliable like the stem, needy as the roots digging in the dirt to feed on the very marrow of life.

Soul is a storyteller that unravels its tale through acts of art. When soul is stifled it creates a restlessness that irritates me into art. When I follow its lead and create, I am rewarded.

I learned long ago that I could be artsy or artful. Artsy is not bad, but like craft, it is about the outer world. It decorates and garnishes and makes pretty, but it lives shallowly. Artful lives deep, rooted in the dimensions of soul.

With artful, the result may not be pretty, but it is always beautiful. I saw clearly the difference between pretty and beautiful as my mother aged. I remember pictures of her as a young woman, very pretty, classic Italian. She was forty-two when I was born. Like so many little boys, I thought she was the prettiest woman in the world. I watched as she turned sixty, seventy, and then eighty. Her prettiness slipped away and a new beauty was born. The old possess a beauty chiseled by life that youth cannot touch. My mother became that beauty.

Artful recognizes the beautiful, even in the absence of pretty. Such beauty can be found in gardens and junkyards alike. My friend Nick, a talented artist, combs junkyards for bits and pieces of material, a length of wire or an old pipe, things that I would never look at twice. I've been with him on these excursions, and while I am crawling to leave he is a little boy in a toy box. He takes his finds home and makes outstanding art works from them, his contribution to recycling and alchemy.

At times I love to be artsy. I love the style and panache. It's like plastic beads at Mardi Gras. But to maintain the health of my soul I need to engage in artful, too. I wonder if one who has a mathematician's soul has the same need to be mathematical.

Flower arranging fulfills the need of the soul for artful. As we work with the myriad of blossoms, inhale their fragrances, dance with their stems, and regale ourselves in nature's ephemeral jewels, we are immersed in the experience of the artful and soul systemically flows through us, encouraging us to our blossom.

In turn soul moves through our flower arrangements as we sink a daisy in the depths or create a meandering line with ivy, or center the arrangement with the chaos of interlocking twigs. Flower arrangements hold their own humor as flowers create sharp contrast and they enjoy their own conviviality as the form gives a sense of camaraderie and belonging to each individual blossom.

While flower arranging as a profession gave me the opportunity to be artful through its rigorous discipline, soul reminds me that every day there is an abundance of opportunities for artful experiences.

The soul recognizes that the art produced, such as a flower arrangement or a poem, does not need to be a masterpiece to have fulfilled its purpose, because its purpose is the process where strength is built and potential fulfilled. By engaging in acts of art we follow the call of our souls, live our purpose, and come to our blossom just as a lotus fulfils its purpose, and blossoms in its time.

Chapter Twenty-four

Vulnerability

W hen I die, I am taking a list of questions with me to heaven, questions for God. First I will inquire about the well-being of my mom, dad, and many others. Then I'm going to ask why He created ugliness. I do not like ugliness; it offends me and even though I make my share of it, including at times, attitudes, words, actions, and on occasion, even an ugly arrangement, I would prefer to live without it.

It becomes especially abhorrent to me when I am the object of other people's ugliness. I was always a big boy and many people, wrongfully believing that people of size are lazy and lack character, consider it their moral obligation and mission to confront large people with this information.

I graduated from Floral Technology and Design in Wichita, KS, on the Thursday before

Easter in 1972. Our instructor suggested that we immediately approach flower shops and let them know that we were available to work through the holiday weekend. I followed his suggestion unaware that that was terrible advice. The busy florists were more annoyed with the unnecessary interruption than interested in more help. In spite of their cool reception, and with a great deal of enthusiasm to begin my new life, I searched for work on foot and by bus.

Needless to say I did not find any opportunities for immediate employment. However the owner of one of KC's largest shops invited me back for an interview on the following Monday. That was an unusual Easter in the Midwest because we had snow. The snow that fell on Thursday still covered the ground Monday when I went to my interview. Excited about the prospect of my first job as a florist, and terribly nervous, I trudged through the snow to the flower shop.

When I arrived there, the gentleman greeted me and requested that I make an arrangement. Shaking from the cold and from nervousness, I made my arrangement. It was terrible. The gentleman owner looked at my work and dismissed me immediately. Then as I was leaving he told me that I was a fat lazy slob who would never make it as a florist, and suggested that I look for other kinds of employment. I trudged on from his flower shop, disappointed but with my determination undaunted. In spite of his ugly opinion and bad manners, I knew I was going to be a florist.

When we feel hurt from someone's attack, they have reached our vulnerability. Vulnerability, a chamber in our souls, can be a dead end or a passageway. Many poems are never written, many paintings never painted, many flowers never arranged, because the artist faced vulnerability, met terror or pain, and stopped. Rather than being stopped, we must move through vulnerability if we are to share the art of our souls.

However, by becoming vulnerable we do not have to leave ourselves defenseless in the face of other people's ugliness. I have developed a strategy to protect my vulnerability, even as I remain vulnerable. As the saying goes, the best defense is a good offense.

We are most at risk when we give more credence to the thoughts and feelings of others than to our own. Their opinions are neither the truth of our souls, nor the reality of our art. They are simply their opinions. The alpha and the omega of our art are our own souls.

So a first line of defense is to prioritize the messages of our own souls about our acts of art. They will give us the most accurate coin of value for our work in relationship to our growth and expression as artists. After we listen to those messages then we can use the helpful lessons and insights from others and discard the rest.

125

This lesson came home a few years ago. I stumbled into a coffee shop where auditions were being held for a play. I was asked to audition. I did so and was cast in a small, fun role. As a result of that role I became a member of that little theater troupe. My peers were recent graduates of theater at University of Missouri, Kansas City, and a few midlife folks who loved performing.

After that play I was again invited to audition with them for a role in Jean-Paul Sartre's *No Exit.* Since it had only four characters I was certain I would not be cast, but I auditioned just for the fun of it. I was flabbergasted when George, the director, asked me to take one of the roles. In spite of feeling intimidated I enthusiastically accepted the role.

My fellow actors and I were on the stage for the entire length of the play. Carrying that role was excruciatingly difficult, but I loved the work. In rehearsals I felt vulnerable and at times I threw temper tantrums. George and the others were patient with me and diligently assisted me in developing the character.

Each night during the run of the play we had our ups and downs, but we played to sold out houses and we received accolades for our work. A review was published in one of the local papers. We received a good review with one exception, me. The reviewer did not care for the way I played my character. George and my fellow cast members were worried about my reaction to the review so we discussed it. In fact I was thrilled with the review and the critic offered some valuable insight into my character. I discerned both the information that was usable as well as the parts of his opinion that were wrong. Neither mattered greatly to me. What did matter was that I saw my name in print in a theater review. I had done the work! After twenty-five years without theater, I was there again and I loved it. The review only made the experience more real and more exhilarating.

Our production was so popular that we extended the run and continued to play to sold out houses. My vulnerability was exposed but protected throughout that experience, because I was listening first to the messages of my own soul. Those messages gave me the true value of the experience.

Another way of protecting our vulnerability is by keeping our work in perspective. Seldom is success defined by one single work, but each individual act of art is another step in the exploration and development of our artist soul. When I lose this perspective I fail to love my work, seeing it only with my critical eye, which always demands perfection as it searches for flaws.

In high school I wrote a series of poems. I showed them only to Aunt Rose, a soul mentor, and herself a poet. Her response to my poetry was both accepting and encouraging. However, I felt so exposed and vulnerable that after she returned the poems, I immediately burned them. So young, I had no perspective on my work, but since then I have had many misfires, projects I'd rather forget, writings best burned, and flower arrangements for my eyes only, but each of those projects was an expression of my artist soul, and each was a moment when the lotus unfurled a petal, if only just a little. So those projects too have their honor. Our creative lives are seldom summed up in a single act of art. When we consider that each act of art is just another moment in a life of creativity, our vulnerability is better shielded.

We also protect our vulnerability by taking ownership for our acts of art. These acts are the messages of our artist souls, so the words are our choice. Perhaps to others they may sound like notes off pitch, but for us they are our voices finding pitch.

My third flower shop job was at Luther's Crestwood Flowers, a lovely neighborhood shop that catered to a more upscale clientele than the first two. Orlan Luther, the owner, took me under his wing, encouraging me to learn and to become my best. One of my chores was to process the flowers when they arrived from the wholesale market. I opened the boxes, removed damaged foliage and petals from the flowers, cut the stems, and put them in water. That task usually took three to four hours. Many days Mr. Luther came to the basement where I worked and we engaged in long, enjoyable conversations. Frequently on Saturday mornings we met at the flower shop at 6 am and headed to the farmers market to forage for fresh fruits, vegetables, and other goodies.

This was still early in my career and the experience at the other shops had not given me the ability to make the quality of arrangements Mr. Luther insisted on for his shop. However he was patiently teaching me his ways and he encouraged me to learn all that I could from the other designers. The design team included his daughter Bonnie, and their close friend, Frankie. Those two were incredible designers and taught me a lot.

But the job had its moments. One late afternoon a family came in and placed an order for a dozen flower arrangements for a funeral that needed to be delivered yet that day. Mr. Luther wanted everything to be perfect. Since there was a time crunch he decided that for the first time in his shop, I could do one of the funeral arrangements. He left the selection of the flowers to me. At the time almost every funeral arrangement had gladiolas, so I chose yellow gladiolas, yellow chrysanthemums and red carnations. We were all standing at the same table making our arrangements yet no one informed me that I was committing a cardinal sin.

When all the work was completed Mr. Luther was looking everything over and noticed my arrangement. He gasped in frustration, brought me the arrangement, and informed me that red and yellow were never to be used together. I don't remember the fate of that arrangement, whether he trashed it, slipped it out on another order, or dismantled it and used the flowers in other arrangements. He was a frugal man so I suppose the latter was the destiny of my arrangement. However, I remembered his lesson in color theory and did not put red and yellow in the same arrangement for years.

Then one day I was standing in my own flower shop, mindlessly making an arrangement. When I had completed it I realized that I had blended red and yellow in the same arrangement. This time I was the one who gasped. Then a thought went through me like lightning. I was now the designer owner of my flower shop and if I liked red and yellow together, which I did, the arrangement was fine. What I had heard in Mr. Luther's comment was that yellow and red together was bad. The truth was that on that day either Mr. Luther did not like yellow and red together or he knew that his customer would not like it. In my shop I took ownership for my act of art.

We must always keep in mind that we first and foremost engage in acts of art for the encouragement, enrichment, and fulfillment of our own artist souls.

Sharing the work of our souls is frightening. It may go unappreciated, disliked, or worse, it may go unnoticed; for some, even our best is never good enough so sharing our art at times brings unjust criticism, even defiant antagonism, but our souls mature through such experiences.

If we forever hide in fear of the possible pain that comes from sharing our vulnerability, we will bring no gifts to the community. Instead we stymie our growth; we slam closed the door to the appreciation of others for our gifts; and we lessen the soul of the community. The vitality and health of the community is dependent on the presence of the gifts of the individual members, not on the perfection of the pieces, but on the good that is shared.

There are times, however, when all attempts to protect my vulnerability fail and again I feel stabbed. Then I console myself by remembering that tears renew the swamp, and that from the swamp the lotus blooms.

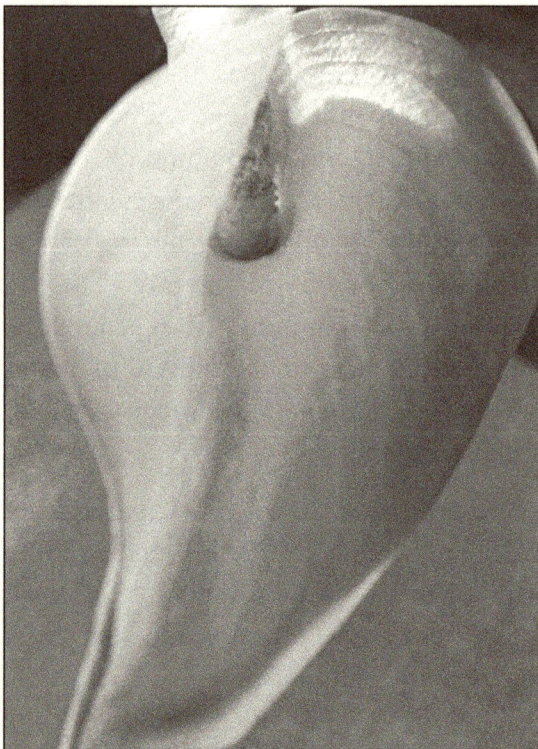

Calla Lily

Chapter Twenty-five

The Creative Core

For a long time I carried around in me an agonizing feeling of emptiness. Then one day I was doing what I call my intuitive doodles and dribbles. I had a large selection of colored markers and a drawing pad. I put on soft music and meditated for a while after which I began doodling until I found the words to write a short poem. I love to make space in my life for this to happen because this practice always leads me on a tour of my inner life.

One day a flower sprouted from a colorful array of lines and squiggles. I then wrote, "Deep in the mire, out of touch, seemingly of no importance because of its distance from the surface, through the dark hole of my past, my pain, my lost loves, all disappointments and damaging experiences, lies my most fertile field, that was almost lost for all times." At that moment I passed through the "hole" and stood at the core of my being. I stood there as certainly as I stand at the front door of my home when I am entering or leaving. I knew that that place was not a region of dead emptiness; rather it was my inner womb, the center of my creativity. I now honor my emptiness because it will bid me to create. And when I create through an act of art I honor my creative core.

When I create an arrangement, I want to be sure I have listened to my intuition. I'll often ask myself, *Have I queried my imagination and allowed it to roam through its world of possibilities? Am I ready to share my voice in my flower arrangement? Have I listened to the needs, wants and desires of whom the arrangement is for? In other words, have I accepted the challenge to create?*

Not every arrangement has to be a masterpiece, but each arrangement can maintain integrity as an act of art. By maintaining creative integrity we grow through our art, one arrangement at a time.

One of the great paradoxes of art, if we are steadfast, is that the art itself will take us to our creative core, that holy of holies where our individual goodness and truth reside. And there lies the seed of our creativity – the seed that holds the essence of our art just as the yet to sprout seed in the mud holds the essence of the lotus.

Chapter Twenty-six

Passion

I enjoy four great passions in life, art, eros, spirituality, and flowers. They are not separate. Like strands in a wreath, they weave themselves together in my imagination and in my soul. They are the roots of the lotus and my reason for being and they called me to be an artist.

If not for passion, my story would be one of a seed lost in the swamp, never finding a way through the mud's confusion. But passion lured me into acts of creation, even as the murky mud obscured my way.

Our passions are what motivate us, rallying us to life and propelling us on our way. As we follow our passions they chart our destinies and they insist we investigate our potential to enjoy depth, intensity, meaning, and bliss. They demand that we explore the glory of life and they lead us to moments of awe. Like a joy ride in a '58 Chevy convertible on a spring day, the pursuit of passion thrills our souls as we become lost in the playground of life, playing with colors, thrilling to flowers, making melodies.

Passion ignites the artist's soul like a match to an oil lamp. The underpinning of the creative life, passion absorbs inspiration and inflames imagination. In our passion lies our promise like a seed in the soil.

In my preteen years, I began hanging out in flower shops. Directly behind our parish church was Edna's. After decades of being in their little shop, Edna, her husband John, and an employee named Tom had devised a unique system for handling orders. I loved to watch their little ritual. During quiet times they would sit and chat. When the telephone rang, Edna stood, answered the phone, and took the order. Next John got up from his chair and selected Edna's container and her flowers. John sat back down while Edna made the arrangement. With the arrangement complete and the card on the bow, she sat back down. Tom then swept the floor and delivered the flowers. Within a very short time they would all again be sitting in their chairs, having light conversation and waiting for the next telephone call.

The hours I spent in flower shops introduced me to the practice of flower arranging and the basics of floristry. I watched the florists sell flowers and make arrangements. I listened to their discussions and learned their likes and dislikes. Passion flowed as they talked about the flowers and the people that purchased them. They were excited for the brides, saddened by the grief of families saying goodbye to loved ones, hopeful for someone receiving their arrangements in the hospital. As a young boy, I was enthralled by their world and by their ability to create those beautiful arrangements and I was always happy to take home some of the leftovers.

At home, I had already put together my first flower shop. I had collected vases, wire and other miscellaneous supplies for my pretend shop and for flowers, I had a seasonal assortment of plastic posies culled from the limited displays at the local TG&Y store. My inventory included roses and carnations in an assortment of colors, Easter lilies and poinsettias, yellow, pink and white daisies, philodendron and ivies. I created arrangements for my room, the house and for Aunt Rose, who lived upstairs. I received *Corsage Craft,* my first book about flower arranging from my parents when I was in fourth grade. From this book I began learning some basics of the craft as it instructed to pull the stem wrap taut and to use the lightest weight wire possible lest the corsage feel like a bowling ball. As I became somewhat proficient I made certain that every woman in the family had a corsage for each holiday.

However, by the time I finally became a florist I was oblivious to my passion's underlying motivation. Lost in the confusion of the growing-up years, I initially went blindly to flowers because of memories of childhood fantasy when I frequented flower shops and pretended to be a florist.

Then, as I slowly awakened, I heard passion's call for a life in art. Flower arranging provided a way to explore and express that call. Anything less than work in a creative arena would have been a renunciation of soul's call.

As passion stirs us to find the genuine work of our souls, it is also calling us to make an individual contribution to the soul of the community, because, like the lotus that needs a swamp, no one exists in isolation.

One time I designed a wedding for a close friend's daughter, who also had become a treasured friend over the years. Just before the wedding my friend introduced me to a family member, commenting on our long friendship and explaining that I had designed the flowers for the wedding. The relative exclaimed, "Oh, I could tell some one had arranged the flowers who really cared." When we follow our passion and create, the effect is visible. This is the presence of soul.

For a time, I held two mistaken beliefs concerning passion. First, in my more naïve years I believed that by following passion I would find the *easier* way. Secondly, when the road became difficult, I believed that by following my passions, I had taken a wrong turn. I have laid those beliefs to rest. Life is a mixed bag, no matter our choices, but when we choose to follow our passions we are choosing diamonds over rhinestones. Many times throughout the years and in spite of any difficulties along the way, by following my passions, I have experienced deep satisfaction, roaring laughter, surprising creativity, and buoying fulfillment

By following my passion for flowers, I have been blessed to be a part of magic moments and special rituals.

My rewards for following my passions into a life with flowers have been many. The tears of a bride when she first sees her bouquet, grateful hugs, letters of thanks, referrals. I have met people through my flower arranging who are now lifetime friends. Some of the joys have even been reaped years after the event. One Sunday afternoon I was at a concert at Grace and Holy Trinity Cathedral in Kansas City when a young lady rushed up to me and exclaimed, "Aren't you Kevin who had the flower shop on Main St.?" "Yes," I replied. "Well you may not remember me, but several years ago you did my wedding flowers and they were wonderful." I greeted this message with joy, and it did not hurt that I was with friends who were also hearing the accolade. She continued, "I loved my bouquet so much that I had it preserved and it sits under glass on my coffee table. I got rid of the groom, but I kept the bouquet!" Such are the joys of being a flower arranger.

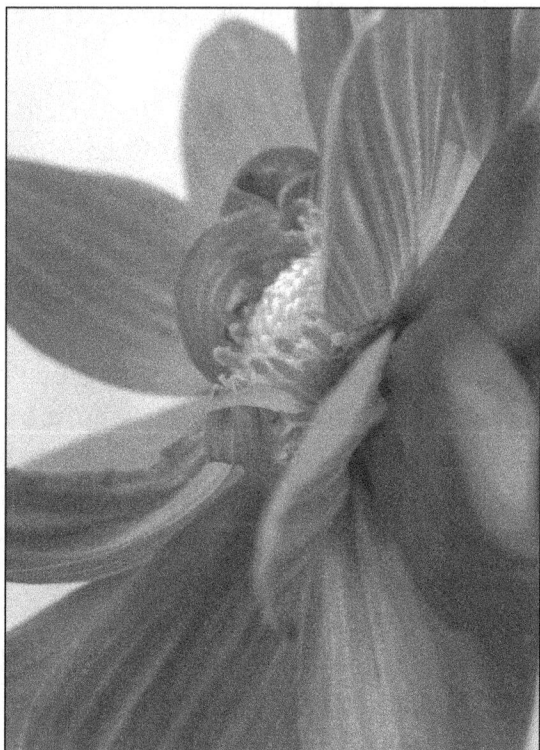

Dahlia

Chapter Twenty-seven

Art's Value

In parochial grade school, some of the nuns taught that work was a punishment from God, first dished out to Adam because he ate an apple. Is it any wonder it's difficult for me to choose an apple over a chocolate bar for a snack! Even had the nuns' messages escaped me, which they didn't, my parents' lessons came through loud and clear. Often for punishment I was forbidden to play and instead sent to clean my room.

Those lessons confused me about the relationship of work and play. They made the two seem like disconnected, polar opposites. Later I came to discover that the two are not so far apart and that work, at its best, is the highest form of play. Work, like play, can be satisfying, even intoxicating, as it transforms the lessons of play into purposeful acts. As a child I played by making flower arrangements and pretended that they decorated altars and were carried by brides. As an adult, at work, I make arrangements that decorate altars and that are carried by brides. Work intensifies the joy, satisfaction, and fulfillment of play, as it gives meaning to the tasks because they are performed to care for ourselves and those we love. Both work and play are among the blossoms of life.

Play and work are exquisitely married in acts of art. The spirit of play and the purpose of work unite to make a union that allows the soul its liberty. But this liberty can be difficult to appreciate because so many of our feelings about work are tied into our experiences with our jobs. In this modern world, jobs are essential sources of income for most of us, and too often they leave us feeling enslaved to the grind. In turn these feelings can alienate us from a soulful relationship with work. However work is done many places: at home, with friends, in volunteer organizations; and for many reasons besides making money. When we can remember the relationship of soul and work, we can come to a deeper understanding of our jobs and soul.

Also, our feelings about money can stymie the purpose of art and confuse its value. Professional artists can easily confuse the reason for engaging in acts of art with the necessity of making a living. If we're not careful, art's true value is lost, and we discount or reject our art based on a bottom line analysis of dollars and cents. And in reverse, art can become appreciated not for itself or for the process but for its price tag.

My all-time favorite artist was Elizabeth "Grandma" Layton. She stands as a great example of someone who found and shared art's true value. Grandma Layton suffered manic depression for years. Neither drugs nor psychotherapy gave her long-term relief. At sixty-eight, Grandma Layton took a contour drawing class where she began doing self-portraits using contour drawing. As she stared in a mirror, she drew herself and her world. Grandma Layton recovered from her depression as she expressed her feelings and insights about the people and issues important to her. These included her husband, family, aging, dieting, death, the ERA, AIDS, and capital punishment.

I love Grandma Layton's energetic drawings and I never miss a chance to see an exhibit of them. On a pleasant Sunday afternoon in April of 1992 I went to an exhibit of her work at the Unitarian Church in Kansas City. By this time Grandma Layton was a significant source of inspiration for me.

As I walked home from the show, dazed by her work, I craved to tell her the impact she had had on me. I wrote to her as soon as I returned home. Besides telling her how I felt about her and her art, I followed an intuitive nudge and requested a doodle, any scribble that she might be willing to share with me. I was earnest in my request and I would have been grateful for some pen scratches that she made while trying to get the ink of a ballpoint pen to flow again. It wasn't that I was unwilling to buy one of her drawings, I would have hawked the home to have one, but she never sold them and I didn't posses the courage to ask her for an actual drawing, even though that's what I wanted most. Also following another deep desire, I asked her if I could visit her. I took my letter to the post office that evening. The following Wednesday I received a letter back. Here is an excerpt:

"Thanks for your beautiful letter...I got your letter Tues and drew this for you last night after supper. The flowers are an azalea potted plant that sets on my desk. About your second request. I have a problem with people coming long ways to visit. I urge those people to go visit the old lady who lives closest to them—she and I are just alike. We all have the same feelings, though naturally about different things. We do have a common bond...Your decision on heroes is just right – it is an every day man striving to do the best he can...If you go by Wellsville some day on the way to somewhere more distant, stop by and say hi.

With love, Elizabeth"

Enclosed with the letter was a beautiful self-portrait with an azalea and a rainbow just behind her smiling face. Receiving her gift was one of the most magical moments in my life. I felt I was given the pearl of great price and I marveled that she was so generous to make a drawing just for me. This experience touched me deeply.

Grandma Layton died less than a year later in March of 1993. I never met her because I did not make the trip "to somewhere more distant" until after her death, but I went to her memorial service at the art center in Lawrence, Kansas, where people displayed drawings she had given them. The walls of the art center were covered with dozens and dozens of her drawings. Each of those drawings, just like mine, was a gift to someone who had been intimately touched by this humble artist. Tears rolled down my cheeks as I met her soul in those drawings. She was a great lady and she taught a lot about the real value of art. Following her death, the majority of her work was bequeathed to the Smithsonian, which continues to show her work at home and abroad.

Years later, I went to Wellsville, Kansas, and visited with her daughter. When we talked about Grandma Layton's generosity with her drawings, she told me that her mother felt she was sufficiently supplied with earthly goods and that her art was one of her ways of giving something back in gratitude for a good life.

Grandma Layton demonstrated the true value of art. First, she showed how art could facilitate a road through suffering. It can give expression to pain just as it can to joy, love, and every other human emotion and condition. And it can be an ingredient in the cure. Because of her inspiring life, innumerable people have used art as a tool to deal with their own suffering.

Secondly she showed through her generosity how priceless art can be when it is freely given. It has been a long time now since I have been to an exhibition of Grandma Layton's drawings, but every day I see the special drawing that hangs in my living room and I am reminded of the example of her generous spirit and I feel encouraged to live intimately through my art. Grandma Layton demonstrated that art at the grass roots shares intimately the goodness of life person to person and neighbor to neighbor.

Valuing art is a conundrum for many artists. We must find ways to earn a living and continue to create. For some, the solution is in earning their money through their art. For others earning money and creating art are completely separate. Some realize celebrity status and earn huge sums for their works, while others sell nothing.

I don't know how to place a monetary value on art, but I am certain that money says nothing about the quality of the intimate conversation coming from an artist's soul. After all art is the conversation of the soul and the soul has no price tag. The most truthful coin of art's value is the integrity of the conversation. An arrangement of flowers picked from the garden and composed with compassion or a painting painted and given in celebration has as much soul value as any other piece of art in existence.

The promise of the Lotus is the freeing of the soul to live and work according to its nature, replenished by the sustenance it draws through its roots. When we live in integrity with our art and our soul's conversation we learn to draw from life the sustenance for our daily bread. Creating art is an act of faith that the works of our souls belong to the swamp of life and that our well being is protected by the honesty with which we approach our lives, living not in the shelter of the certainty of plenty, but in the ability to create more as is needed. This is not the way of ease, but the challenge of the swamp so that in our time we may bloom from our souls, even if at times we first sink into the mud.

Chapter Twenty-eight

Home

Creating art is not simply an act but a way of life. In order to have the inner substance from which to create, we need to nurture our roots and feed our psyches. For this reason, as an apple needs a tree, artists need a strong sense of rootedness, a sense of home.

I know that my home is a cocoon for my soul where I engage in deep dreams and vivid imaginings. Relaxed at home, my soul holds court with my thoughts and feelings, and traipses through the terrain of my reflections.

Our souls need cocoons where they feel safe and nurtured. Too often in the world they feel like orphans, so we must feed, clothe and shelter them in ways that sustain them and let them know that they belong just as the lotus belongs to the swamp.

I have cultivated a home that nurtures my soul and pampers my senses. Each room is similarly furnished with an eclectic accumulation of loved heirlooms, souvenirs from my travels, treasured gifts from friends, pieces from my junking, and art I have found irresistible. I often bought art when I didn't have enough money for groceries.

My friend, Debbie, calls my home "Kevin's mini art museum," and I love her description, because it describes a place where treasures are cherished and from the time I walk in my front door my treasures surround me.

I love to enter my home through the front door and scan the cozy living room. At the far end is a blue and white striped love seat with Victorian-styled flower cushions, and across from it is a big comfy navy blue leather chair, which I jokingly call my throne, where I sit when I visit with guests, read, meditate, or watch my fish swimming in the aquarium that sits on a Victorian marble top washstand. Scattered around the room are three antique chairs, a Victorian side chair, an Italian side chair and a generic old chair, with a high back, wooden arms and legs, and the original, now-faded burgundy upholstery. I love this shabby chair, a birthday gift from Aunt Evelyn and Aunt Rose over thirty years ago.

On the back of the chair I drape a small, handloomed rug made and given to me by my friend Bill as a sympathy gift when my mother died. Each time I look at that rug I remember the moment at the funeral home when he arrived, carrying it in a brown grocery bag, and handed it to me with a big bear hug. His presence and gift were salve for my aching soul. When I see it I am warmed by the memories of the love that held me up and carried me through such a difficult time.

Beside the loveseat is an antique kneeling bench that doubles as both an end table and a pedestal for a nineteenth-century French brass candelabra. The candelabra with its filigree crosses on the base probably began its life in a church or chapel, perhaps a private chapel in a French villa. Often as I look at it, I imagine it on a stone altar with just a few chairs, a simple communion rail and saints on pedestals to keep watch.

On the wall next to the kneeling bench hangs a lithograph by Seelig that whimsically depicts the seventh day of creation, with Eve swinging in a hammock as Adam watches on. Hanging above that is a watercolor of people strolling the Champ Elysees, which reminds me of a few beautiful autumn days when I too, strolled the streets of Paris. Above the love seat in a gilded frame hangs a watercolor painting by a Russian artist depicting three jesters dancing. I love the archetypal image of the court jester who was often the most influential person in the court because, through his humor, he could tell the truth to the king. A good lesson about truth telling.

On the opposite side of the love seat from the kneeling bench is a small pedestal rescued from the trash by my friend Shirley. When she laid eyes on it she knew it would find a home in my house. On it is a 36" tall carving of an African man. It had its origins in the Ivory Coast, but I purchased it at a flea market in Berkeley from a man who traveled between California and Africa buying and selling his wares.

That flea market is part of a Saturday ritual that I enjoy whenever I visit San Francisco. First I go to that funky old flea market, which is held in the parking lot at one of the BART (train) stations. Then I saunter over to Telegraph Avenue, where I forage through all the great little shops and boutiques that line the street. I stop for coffee several times along the way to relish the rich deep roast coffees of the Bay Area. I always end my little field trips on the Berkeley Campus of the University of California, where each Saturday afternoon there is a drumming circle.

On the Saturday that I bought the African carving, my ritual went as per usual, except that I was carrying this very large art piece, its head poking out the top of a black plastic trash bag. Needing to find a men's room after so much coffee, I went into one of the campus buildings. When I left, I went to the drumming circle, and since I was without a drum, I just sat, listened, and became absorbed in the invigorating rhythms.

While sitting there, totally lost in the bold intense drumming, two police officers walked up to me. It seemed that someone had seen me carrying that statue out of the campus building and reported me for possible art theft. The officers took information and ran checks on me, detaining me there for about an hour before letting me go. Each time I look at that carving, I chuckle at the memory of that humorous afternoon. A piece of wood so filled with memories – this is the sort of thing that connects us to soul.

Near the African carving is another pedestal, one of a pair that my friends Charles and John crafted for me as a thank you for the flowers I arranged for their holy union. On that pedestal is a three-branch wrought-iron candelabra rich in detail. This piece was given to me by my friend Joe as an appreciation gift for the arrangements I had created for his father's funeral.

Also in my living room there is a corner china cabinet, a Georgian bookcase, and a nineteenth-century French baker's rack, with Hummel figurines, a wood carved Crèche, a rather jolly wooden Buddha, books, and other miscellaneous knickknacks. My 1890 upright piano is also covered with art objects and candles. The walls are covered with paintings and art pieces in European gallery fashion.

The floors are hardwood and the only rug is a contemporary Chinese throw rug in front of the love seat and on which sits my mother's coffee table. Off to the side beside my old chair there is a companion table. Both tables are intricately carved rose wood from Italy left to me by my parents. I was in my early twenties when they told me they wanted me to have those tables someday. Since my love for antiques and other beautiful things had been obvious since I was a little boy they knew I would appreciate them. One day while I was visiting them, dad told me about their decision regarding the tables, and even as he was saying it I saw the lights flash on in his head. On the spur of the moment he decided I should not wait but instead I should carry them home that very day. Then my mother intervened. She confirmed that it was also her wish that I have those tables some day, but she warned my father that if he didn't stop trying to give away her belongings, the only thing that would be carried out of the house that day would be him! Twenty plus years later I carried those tables home wishing that I could have waited at least another twenty years before I needed to take possession of them.

My belongings are not an accumulation set in place to impress, rather they are treasures that feed my imagination, soothe my spirit, and seduce me into involvement with my deepest dreams. I love being at home where I've made places that comfort my body, stimulate my mind, and pleasure my senses.

Whether a home is one room or a mansion, it is a hideaway and workshop where we can with-

draw from the world and be at play. We can rearrange to our hearts' content, as we bring in the
new, throw out the used up, rejuvenate the sag-
ging. There we can relish the old and indulge in
memories. We can experiment with our ideas,
letting our creativity be our guide. Our homes
are places where we can love our families, our
guests, and ourselves extravagantly and home is
where we care for our ordinary selves.

At home we take off our public self, like
muddy shoes. It's where we flip-flop to the
kitchen in our pj's to imbibe our first morning
cup of coffee. It is where we brush our teeth, cut
our toenails, graze in the refrigerator, leisurely
work a crossword puzzle, read books, and watch
TV. For those of us who live with others, it is
where we nurture the intimacy of our primary
relationships and for those of us choosing to live
alone, it is where we relish our solitude.

Home is where we most consistently pamper
our souls by the attention we give to our ordinary
selves. This is another lesson of the Lotus, because from its ordinary roots, stems, and leaves,
comes its extraordinary blossom.

Daisy

Chapter Twenty-nine

Artist Block, Artist Sleep

I love to traipse to the wholesale flower market, shopping for the flowers to fill each of my orders. We are fortunate in Kansas City to have several viable and competent wholesale houses but my favorite destination is Koehler and Dram, where my friends Kay and Paul are at the helm and where I worked part time for many years. Several of my other former co-workers are still there, so I use my shopping expeditions as an excuse to check in and chat with each of them. The enduring friendship of these good people has been a grace note in my life.

On these excursions, besides socializing, I meander through their coolers to make my selections. There are five in all, one with boxed flowers waiting to be processed, one with only greens, and one with tropical flowers including a variety of orchids, gardenias, protea, antherium, ginger and birds of paradise. Another is devoted to roses, carnations, poms, spider mums, cremons, mini carnations, and gladiolas all in a rainbow of colors. The largest cooler displays buckets of delphinium, larkspur, Queen Anne's lace, acacia, heather, tulips, iris, hydrangea montbretia, asters, alstromeria, lilies, freesia, liatrice, statice, stars of Bethlehem, bouvardia, and many others, some I don't know by name. I walk through the coolers and imagine combinations I might make before I settle on the ones I will take with me. I spend an inordinate amount of time with this little exercise because of the pleasure I receive as I look at all the flowers and imagine arrangements.

There are times, however, when my imagination seems withered, my creativity as dry as a creek in a drought and none of the flowers in the coolers spark any ideas. Those are mostly the times when I am experiencing artist block.

Artists' block, a state of mind that comes to nearly all artists at one time or another, is distinguished by feeling uninspired, frustrated, dry, numb, disenchanted. If we are honest with ourselves we are feeling a little less than alive. Artists often summon all the muses and angels of heaven in an attempt to battle and to defeat this beast.

The very term "artists' block" denotes a dead end. It can feel very threatening until we gain an understanding that these "blocks" are far more than a state where nothing creative happens. They have their own purpose in the creative cycle. That's why I like to call them "artists' sleep." This gives poetic understanding to the barren periods and seizes upon them as opportunities to rest, recoup, and recover and to dream again. Just as Shakespeare said, "To sleep, perchance to dream."

I used to love to sleep, whether in my cozy bed at night or in my easy chair for a nap, until my sleep was disrupted with sleep apnea and I went several years with restless nights and few dreams. I came to a point where my agitated, dreamless nights began to seem normal. During that period I started to dread going to bed, because I knew the grueling night ahead and the ugly morning rising that would end it. Then, after I was treated for this, I again enjoyed long nights of deep sleep and the return of my dreams.

Having taken them for granted for so many years and after a long period without them, I came to a whole new appreciation of dreams. I felt as though I had been reunited with old friends.

Our nocturnal dreams allow elements of the mud of life to surface. Like the mud in a swamp, our inner world is filled with both recognizable and imperceptible elements, from which we can draw energy as well as insight.

Even if we never analyze them, dreams still work to revitalize us. As a matter of fact, since

159

dreams are mysterious communications, I most often prefer to leave them whole and to wonder at their mystery, to read them as poetry rather as an owner's manual, to see them as stories to be perused rather than as sentences to diagram. I prefer not to over rationalize the mysterious, because if I leave dreams as dreams and trust the nocturnal work of my soul, I will enjoy the beauty, the pathos, and the comedy of its poetry.

In artist sleep, just as in nocturnal sleep, it looks like nothing is happening, but soul is sifting through the mud at its own leisure, regenerating its enthusiasm and vitality, and finding the bits and pieces it will use in our next storyline. This is not a time to fight, but a time to relax and trust.

In our mechanized world it is tempting to see the soul as just another machine, to be turned on and off at will, as it is required to manufacture a product on demand. But soul has its own cycles, which are patterned more after the seasons than after man's machinery. Soul does not produce on demand; rather it blooms, in its own time and in its own season, and like all of nature, it needs rest.

For a few years, as I mentioned previously, every time I turned around I was going to another funeral. The week my mother died I went to three. That period took a terrible toll.

A month after my mother's death, Uncle Jim, her youngest brother, died. With the weight of those two deaths too much for her to bear, Aunt Evelyn, their sister, collapsed in a nervous break down. Because of our close friendship through the years, I became her primary care giver, looking after her affairs and her care, which included placing her in a retirement home for the last four years of her life. She never regained her strength or her mental well-being and those last years of her life were excruciating for her and for me.

After her death, I felt completely spent, wanting only to get on a slow boat to nowhere and just ride, preferably for years. Fortunately she had left me a small sum of money that allowed me to take some time away. I traveled a bit and hid out at home some. But I also needed to earn a living, since my inheritance was not sufficient to sustain me for long. Hoping to find something that would supplement my design studio, I tried different jobs, including an ill-fated office job and another position as a floral designer. However, one of the great difficulties during that time, was that I felt that my artist soul had withered and that I no longer wanted to arrange flowers. To make matters worse, when I did take jobs with other florists I felt robbed of my last shreds of energy.

My soul was in its sleep mode. I no longer wanted to do anything creative, and while I was still able to respond when necessary, with appropriate arrangements, I took no joy in the work. Artist sleep can be difficult, as can the events that lead to it, but there is a brooding beauty in the night when the soul seeks rest, whether we enter the darkness kicking and screaming or crawl in surrender like a child worn out from play.

Perhaps the greatest difficulty in entering artist sleep is that we face the death of desire. Desire is that gentle craving, that tender yearning, which seduces us to pursue the act of creation. Ignored, desire atrophies, or in the other extreme, it is obliterated when drowned in over consumption of the object of its desire. But when we allow our souls to rest, desire will be reborn as we dream.

Artists must be attentive to the messages of the soul during the dream times, lest opportunity be missed and the wake up delayed. The first message may be a suggestion to make a small arrangement from the bouquet of flowers at the super market, or a first line of poetry may slip into our minds, or an idea for a painting may sprout from what seems like nowhere. When I began my awakening from the time I just described, I wrote the first line of this book. If we ignore those first awakenings we run the risk of doing what my mother warned me against, which was "Sleeping my life away."

Recently I made my first spring visit of the year to Powell Gardens with my friend Shirley. We always make a point of going early to see the azaleas in bloom, but this year, because of late freezes, everything is behind the normal calendar cycle so we were there while the gardens mostly still slept. But they were having their first awakening. Interspersed throughout the gardens were thousands of daffodils, hyacinths, tulips, and grape hyacinths. As well, magnolias, forsythia, and redbuds were flickering with their first colors. I had never been to the gardens at a time when so many bulbs were in bloom, so I had no idea of their splendor. What a great surprise! At a distance the woodland garden still seemed muted and asleep, but I noticed the trees were shadowed with a shimmering white and a touch of yellow. As I walked closer I recognized the star magnolias and jonquils, but closer still and I saw the many purple and pink hyacinths, and the redbud trees that were adding delicate colors to a gray palette, the first signs of a voluptuous season yet to come.

This, too, is how the soul awakens from its sleep, first with sparks, and then with an explosion of the full array of its color, but we must be attentive to its early wake-up call and cooperate with its prodding.

The most ordinary moments can encapsulate the most exquisite theater. Through them I experience a new insight or am reminded of an old understanding of the human drama. For many years, I have worked as an official at the polls on Election Day. During one election, I was having a discussion with two of my co-workers, Vi and

Elzeta, when suddenly Vi, who had worked every election since Franklin Roosevelt won his fourth term, began talking about rocking her babies. She spoke softly and lovingly about holding them until they were asleep, and then she would just sit and look at them and admire their beauty. As she told that story, I could see the expression and the love of the young Vi gazing at her babies. Elzeta, agreeing, took on a similar expression as she talked about rocking her own babies.

I felt as though I had been transported to some timeless place filled with mothers' love and I remembered how as a little boy I crawled on the sofa beside my mother and rested my head in her lap and how loved I felt as she stroked my hair and patted my back. And I was reminded of the rest possible for the soul if we trust artist sleep and allow our souls to relax in the lap of life as we take our naps. The lotus sleeps and is reborn to bloom again and we as artists can trust that as we take our naps we too will awaken from our dreams revived, ready to again engage in acts of art.

Chapter Thirty

Beauty

Everyday, if we look, we will find beauty that takes our breath away.

Five o'clock am. I walked from my college room to chapel for Mass. A snowstorm that dumped several inches of snow was still adding more layers. Aware of only a single street lamp lighting my way, I looked down and a rabbit crossed my path leaving paw prints in an otherwise untouched snow.

Dawn in Loose Park, while taking a morning stroll through the rose garden, a melody arose from a single flute.

In the Louvre, standing before Michelangelo's slaves, tears came to my eyes.

Once on a float trip with friends, as we paddled into a cove we spilled. My head bobbed under the water. I came up and saw an exquisite miniature pine tree. Scattered stones lay about it.

At the opera, after a pleasant first act, Renée Fleming came to the stage and sang an aria.

In San Francisco, as I sat on the patio of a café waiting for my dinner the fog rolled in.

In Giverny, I stood on Monet's bridge overlooking his gardens.

In Los Angeles at the Getty Museum, I sat behind a fountain. Between the fountain and myself were willows. I gazed at the branches as they swayed in the breeze to the rhythms of the water.

Pre-dawn on a mountaintop in northern California, I sat on a park bench enveloped in the mists, and then dawn!

These quiet, peak moments allow me to know beauty as a lover knows his beloved. In these intimate moments, all my senses are immersed in beauty and my soul in awe.

I do not create these moments. They are a gift from the gods. They inspire my aesthetic sensibilities and generate my art.

Sadly, we can become so absorbed in the daily soap opera of our lives that we miss paradise. We live on a voluptuous planet in a magnificent universe. Mother Earth is the grandest of all grande dames. She opens her cloak and her beauty cascades like water over the Niagara Falls, bestowing on us her richest jewels and poshest furnishings. What is more beautiful than a bird, a seashell or a flower?

What's more, we can cultivate a relationship with beauty. Like all relationships, this one requires attention, time, and focus. We can welcome its presence in our lives by the surroundings we maintain, the company we keep, and the way we spend our time.

Beauty, like love, is not in the domain of the hurried and frantic. Its consistent gifts arrive in leisure, relaxation, and concentration. A glimpse of an arrangement can get one's attention, but it is through spending time with it that one really comes to know it. We can glimpse the beautiful in haste, but we can only savor it in leisure.

I am never closer to the sacred than when I am in the presence of beauty, but to see it I must keep my eyes open.

In the summer after my freshman year in high school I took a trip to New York City with my father and Jim, his business associate. I had a small savings account, mostly the bounty of Christmas and birthday gifts, plus the earnings from a few odd jobs, so my dad insisted that if I joined the trip I had to pay my own way. After driving for two days with only a few hours sleep in Pennsylvania, we arrived in Manhattan where I indulged in a great all-day tour. The Empire State Building, the Statue of Liberty, lunch in Chinatown, and two traffic jams were among the day's highlights. The next morning we headed for Canada. I was exhilarated by the wonders I had seen.

Along the way I picked up some tourist brochures and discovered that the drive north would take us within a few miles of Niagara Falls, so as soon as we were on the highway, I petitioned for a detour to the falls. Jim said a definite no and my dad, being ambivalent, decided to vote on Jim's side. I was so angry I closed my eyes and kept them closed nearly all the way. Guess who missed the trip! I have never since made that drive, nor will I ever again have the opportunity to share that ride with my father, who shared with me a great love for the beauty of the planet.

All was not lost, though. Those few stubborn hours provided me with an important lesson that I return to again and again, when I am about to close my eyes on beauty because I am angry, sad, or depressed. They instilled in me a reminder to keep my eyes open to beauty always. I treasure beyond words those moments when I know the Elysian Fields. But beyond those moments, I enjoy each and every opportunity I have to find beauty in the simple daily moments where it blossoms.

I think that one of the most joyous gifts given to human beings is the ability to experience beauty. Coupled with that is the ability to take the raw gifts of the earth and to create more beauty in all its forms and through all relationships. This is the gift we flower arrangers share through our art as we scatter morsels of bliss like bread to the birds and create, for ourselves and others, a moment of beauty, a taste of paradise.

Peony

Chapter Thirty-one

The Lotus Blooms

Flower arranging is at home in an ordinary life.

Living an ordinary life is an extraordinary accomplishment, especially today. In a culture that worships celebrities and envies their possessions we can too easily lose our imaginations by dreaming possibilities we can never realize.

But, by engrossing ourselves in our ordinary lives, we allow our imaginations the power to electrify our lives with dreams of all we can be, based in the knowledge of *who we are*. Just as a flower arrangement is born one flower at a time, it is through the ordinary tasks, relationships, moments, and reflections of life that we meet ourselves, enjoy the deliciousness of our lives and come to live truly creative, artful lives.

Through ordinary moments, we scale peaks and descend to the depths. At times when it seems like nothing special at all is happening we are accumulating the riches of an ordinary life. These are the moments of the soul. When the shadow dances with the sun, soul hums the melody. When we climb great heights for lofty views, soul holds the ladder. Soul thrives in the details of our lives.

My friend Shirley and I share a profound love for the sky, relishing its beauty. Often as we drive somewhere one of us will point to it, each of us nearly speechless, because no words adequately describes its glory. Many evenings she has called me at eight, nine or even ten o'clock and told me that I must go look at the moon. So I rush to find my robe and slip into my sandals and head to the backyard to check it out. At times, with the fondness of a child reminiscing about a parade, she will describe a previous night's sky.

Such are the delicious moments that fill an ordinary life. To a casual observer they look insignificant, but they are the building blocks of something extraordinary. It is most often in the ordinary moments of life that we hear soul's call. Still, today, I love walking into a room and seeing a flower arrangement. Sometimes memories flood through me and I am again a little boy sitting beside my mother on our red couch, admiring the roses sent to her by my father. Or I am again an altar boy gazing at the altar flowers during Mass. These are memories of moments in my ordinary life when soul called me to flower arranging.

The world is lush with opportunities to hear soul's call. A child holding a baby may hear the first call to parenthood. Someone caring for a sick friend may hear the call to nursing. A few piano lessons may be the first whispers of a life-long passion for music. The call is heard in moments when enthusiasm thrives, joy bubbles, and love magnetizes. But we must remember that soul's call is also echoed in dark nights and difficult moments. Deep grief from the death of a loved one may be the call to help others facing loss. Anguish from depression may be the call to heal through art. Soul calls us to vocation and avocation alike, to solitude and to relationship. Placing a few garden flowers in a vase may herald the call to flower arranging.

I began this chapter in the middle of December. It seemed like a fitting time to write a final chapter. It was the longest and loveliest autumn in my memory. Even as I was preparing to enter into winter, the temperatures were moderate and we were having many sunny days. The restful dreariness of winter had yet to arrive.

I returned to Squaw Creek to look again at the swamp that is home to thousands of lotuses. I went there expecting to see a barren swamp with only the scraps of summer's blooms remaining. Instead I stared at a gathering of thousands of snow geese that were resting there until the swamp freezes and they move on further south. American bald eagles were perched in the naked trees. I stood in absolute awe and I was reminded that we live in a frugal universe. Nature wastes nothing.

My friend Jude introduced me to the lotus. She told me about how its roots grow in the mud of the swamp bottom, and its stem shoots up strong and sturdy, and breaks through the water. Its radiant flower waves to the heavens.

When I met Jude I was in the winter of my soul. I felt wasted. I could not believe anything could take root in the swamp of my life, let alone a lotus. But we live in a frugal universe and the soul wastes nothing. While the lotus sleeps, the snow geese are fertilizing and renewing the swamp. And in its winter, my soul was sustained by life.

After learning about the lotus from Jude, I decided that if I was going to have to endure the mud of life then I wanted the blossom also. Our lives bloom, not from random chance, but when we follow the calls of our souls.

The glory of the lotus is its blossom. The glory of living is a life in bloom. The blossom is no accident. It is born from a life that is carefully and artfully crafted from the raw materials handed down by life. Our choice is not if something will come from those raw materials, but how artfully we will choose to use them.

The lotus has become a meditation for both my art and my life. Its life cycles give meaning to the suffering and confusion in life, while it also speaks to joy and gratitude. And it shows that in our muddiest moments we can sustain hope by remembering the bloom that is to come.

We creatives possess the ability to bring a different vision to this world. Through the practice of birthing art from chaos, we each hold a ray of vision that allows us to look at the mud of this world and to imagine a lotus in bloom, to look at the chaos and imagine beauty waiting to be born. However to do this we must live with open eyes and open hearts and a willingness to look beyond the communal mud for the potential that soul is calling for the world to live out.

The practice of soulful art is a spirituality of becoming that utilizes the mud and the sunshine alike. This alchemical spirituality places equal emphasis on being and doing, and respects the intricate relationship of the two. The lotus blossoms from the stem, above the leaves, which sprout from the seed that drops from the blossom into the mud. Generations birthing generations. Being and doing, each constantly born and re-born from the other, ever becoming.

Engaging in acts of art is not an adjunct to life. Rather, acts of art are indispensable rituals that are constant reminders of the stages of the lotus. Those stages are the seasons of our lives. If we stay rooted in the mud and remain pointed to the heavens, in season, our lives bloom.

When we approach the act of creating a flower arrangement, we have two basic choices. We can treat it as another hurried project we have to get done in our harried lives. Or we can approach the flowers with attention as we bask in their beauty and reach deep within ourselves to give expression to soul. When we choose the latter, in time, flowers will unfold their quiet wisdom, a blossom within the blossom. Just like the lotus every flower has a story to tell and a lesson to teach, because each is a page in nature's story.

Nature is the first divine story told on earth. And like all good stories, it holds great lessons. But unlike other stories, nature is both the story and the storyteller.

Nature's story enlivens our lives with the breath of spirit and animates our lives with the heart of soul. Soul and spirit, the hands of this embodied life that allow us to touch timeless wisdom and the eternal divine.

Just as the printer facilitates the telling of the story within the pages of a book, flower arrangers facilitate the telling of the flowers' stories for those who would listen. Certainly the lotus tells a magnificent story.

This, then, is the art and this is the soul of flower arranging: To see the empty vase and the scattered flowers and to know the arrangement. This is letting the lotus bloom.

Post Script

Community and Acknowledgements

We are shaped by those we stand in the presence of, just as a rock in the river is shaped by the water.

The alchemy of soul creates community, just as it creates art and artists. Community is born one conversation, one movie, one game, one argument, one walk, one catastrophe, and one triumph at a time.

There was a time when in my misguided perceptions I thought community was about conformity, a group of people so similar in belief or thought that they were bound together by activity, camaraderie, and expression. But community is more like an English garden with its larkspur, foxglove, roses, daisies, yarrow, and delphinium. The diversity of color, shape, size, and purpose, create splendor. There the organizing element is not sameness, but an attempt through nurture and care to help each plant be its best. In community, as in the garden, glory lies in its array of color and blooms and its strength lies in the quality of the individual plants.

Life has gifted me with a vibrant community. Some have been my traveling companions for decades, while others were in my life only briefly. We met in many places and for many purposes; some are still with me and some have gone their separate ways; some have contributed to this book.

First I wish to express my gratitude to Jude Le Claire for introducing the lotus to me. To Anne Hargrove who saw the spark and recognized the flame. To my writer's group who met together for years to support the work, Karen Martin, Lou Sondern, and Gail Harkness. To Mary Hockersmith, Larry Yoder, Carol Gregor, Matthew Carnicelli, Elizabeth Cutting, Louise Tritton, Casey McCabe, Larry Houlton, Willa Cathlina, Jean Moulder and Bill Buck, whose comments propelled this book on. To Maggie Neff who was the right person at the right time to help me take the next step. To Ardith Beveridge for her reflective response and encouragement. To my editor, Caroline Pincus who so artfully helped to sculpt the final draft. To Victoria Moran for support and advice from beginning to end. To Thomas Moore and Joan Hanley. To Tom for his gracious foreword and continuing support of this book and to both of them for opening their home and their hearts to me at a defining moment in my life. To David Biegelsen whose support and photos enhanced this work. To Hugh Adams Russell whose support and encouragement made this book possible. And finally to Shirley Hull and Joseph Cecil whose unwavering support carried me during the dark nights of this writing.

These have been my mentors and my friends. All of these and many more have been my traveling companions on my pilgrimage to the sacred and all of them, while scattered and never together as a unit, are my community and they urge me on to my best, and to my blossom. Together we have shared happiness, sadness, catastrophe, victory, idleness and busyness. They have encouraged, energized, forgiven, and loved me. But more than anything else we have shared conviviality through the pleasure and the joy of living.

On our visits to my grandparents' home in Iowa, I slept in the attic, in the same room where my father and his brothers had slept. This comfortable room had several beds, antique tables, some of my grandmother's knickknacks, some of my grandfather's hunting and fishing paraphernalia, and other bric-a- brac, most of which I have forgotten. But I remember the warmth of the room and the coziness of the iron bed with its super soft mattress, feather pillows, and old tattered comforters. I suspect whoever coined the phrase' "sweet dreams," had also slept in the very same bed or one just like it, because that is what this bed fostered. The coziness of that bed is the coziness of friendship, which wraps us and sustains us through our lives, and keeps us warm as we dream.

At the roots of soulful community lies friendship, which nurtures our souls and encourages us to live to our blossoming. It is in the presence of this community of friends that I stand, and while I am the author of this book, the work that blossoms here is from us.

The publication of this book is made possible by a generous grant from the Charles Bedard Fund.

Kevin Joel Kelly has been a professional floral designer for more than thirty years. Before becoming a florist, Kevin studied in a Catholic Seminary. There both his interest in art and the sacred flourished. He has taught floral design in classrooms to aspiring professionals, one on one in flower shops and in workshops. Kevin lives in Kansas City, MO where he is a freelance floral designer and offers classes and workshops in flower arranging.

To contact the author or to inquire about speaking engagements, classes, workshops or retreats for your group, please write to him at:

7603 Jefferson
Kansas City, MO 64114

Please send a stamped self-addressed envelope.

You can purchase this book at:
www.llumina.com/store/lotusbloom.htm

www.ingramcontent.com/pod-product-compliance
Lightning Source LLC
Chambersburg PA
CBHW031840090426
42741CB00005B/301